Cybersecurity for CEOs

What Every Business Leader Needs to Know

Sean P. Conroy

ISBN: 979-8-9992431-0-2

Library of Congress Control Number: 2025913276

Contents

Introduction

Why Cybersecurity Is No Longer Optional

Ten years ago, most people saw cybersecurity as just an IT issue. Now, it's a boardroom concern, and it's showing up on the CEO's desk.

Cyberattacks have changed. Ransomware can bring a business to a stop in just a few hours. Phishing emails look completely real. And the attackers? They don't need to be tech experts anymore; they can buy a subscription to Ransomware-as-a-Service.

At the same time, regulators, insurers, customers, and investors are all asking more challenging questions. "Are you secure?" isn't just a tech question now; it's a business one. The stakes aren't just about system downtime anymore. They include lawsuits, damaged reputations, and lost customers.

This book is here to shift your mindset from seeing cybersecurity as something you hand off to something you take responsibility for.

If you're a CEO, founder, or executive at a small or midsize business, especially in finance, healthcare, legal, SaaS, or professional services, this book is meant for you.

You don't need to be a technical expert. You need to understand what's at risk, what to ask, and how to lead your team toward better security.

This isn't written for CISOs or security engineers. It's not a technical guide, and I won't teach you how to set up a firewall. This is for leaders who need to get up to speed quickly on how to protect their business.

I know your time is limited. That's why I designed each chapter to be easy to skim and valuable on its own.

Inside, you'll find:

- Stories that show how cyber threats impact small businesses
- Clear explanations of key ideas in everyday language
- Insights aimed at CEOs and executives, focusing on what matters
- Checklists and action steps at the end of each chapter to help you move forward

You don't need to read it from start to finish. Just pick the chapter that fits what you're facing today, and come back whenever you need more.

This isn't just a book. It's a practical tool, and in today's threat landscape, it might be one of the most essential tools in your leadership kit.

Chapter 1

Why Cybersecurity Is Now a CEO Problem

On May 1, 2021, a ransomware attacks crippled a major healthcare company in San Diego, CA.

Overnight, electronic health records went dark. Patient portals were locked. Surgeries were canceled. Ambulances had to be diverted to other hospitals. Doctors and nurses reverted to pen and paper while executives scrambled to respond.

The disruption didn't last a day; it stretched nearly a month.

The total damage amounted to more than $112 million, comprising lost revenue, investigation costs, and recovery expenses. However, the hidden toll ran deeper: patient trust eroded, employee morale suffered, and the reputational fallout spread through the community and the media.

And Scripps wasn't an unprepared organization. They had a cybersecurity budget. They had an IT staff. They weren't careless. However, like many organizations today, they were facing threats that had evolved faster than their defenses and more quickly than their leadership had realized.

If a primary healthcare system with significant resources can be brought to its knees, what does that mean for a growing company with 100 employees and a lean IT team?

This chapter breaks down why cybersecurity is no longer something CEOs can delegate. Because when your business is attacked, you won't just be asked how it happened; you'll be expected to explain why you weren't ready.

The Scripps attack wasn't just a wake-up call for hospitals. It was a warning for every business leader.

In today's world, cyberattacks aren't rare. They aren't random. And they're not limited to large corporations. Small and midsize businesses are now frequent targets. Why? Because they're easier to hit, fewer safeguards, smaller teams, and a mindset that says, "We're too small to matter."

That mindset is dangerous.

Cybercrime has matured into a full-blown industry. Tools like Ransomware-as-a-Service enable low-skilled attackers to rent software, utilize phishing kits, and launch campaigns with ease. It's not a lone hacker in a basement anymore. It's organized, funded, and focused, and your company is just another name on the list.

Some hard truths:

- Ransomware incidents cost small and mid-sized businesses an average of $740,000 per case, excluding downtime, lost revenue, and recovery expenses (Coveware, 2023).
- 71% of security breaches target small businesses (National

Cybersecurity Alliance).

- Regulatory fines and lawsuits are on the rise, particularly in industries that handle sensitive data, such as healthcare, finance, and legal services.

- After a breach, many small to medium-sized businesses (SMBs) lose business from major customers, and some lose contracts altogether.

Even cyber insurance isn't the safety net it once was. Insurers are tightening policies. Claims are denied if you haven't met basic standards, such as multifactor authentication, encrypted backups, or endpoint protection.

The bottom line: whether you have 10 employees or 1,000, a breach lands on your desk. Your IT team can manage the systems, but the responsibility for risk starts and ends with you.

Cybersecurity Has Become a Leadership Responsibility

Cybersecurity used to be a backend issue, something the IT team quietly managed, like printer problems or server maintenance. That world doesn't exist anymore.

Today, cybersecurity is a strategic business risk, right alongside finance, legal, and compliance. And like those areas, it needs executive oversight, not just technical action.

Why does this fall to leadership?

- Only leadership can set priorities and approve the budget.

- Only leadership can ensure accountability across teams.
- Only leadership can establish a lasting security-minded culture.

Handing off security entirely to your IT team is like telling your accountant to "just take care of taxes" and never reviewing your financials. In the end, you're still responsible. And if a breach happens, you'll be the one answering to customers, insurers, and regulators.

Think of cybersecurity the way you think about business insurance. You don't need to understand every clause in the policy, but you do need to know what's covered and what isn't. The same goes here. You don't need to know how to configure a firewall or define a zero-day exploit. But you should be asking:

- Are our data backups resistant to ransomware?
- Can we detect if someone breaks into our systems?
- What would our response be if we were attacked today?

This isn't about turning yourself into a part-time security expert. It's about taking ownership and asking the right questions because no one else can do that for you.

What This Means for You

If you're the CEO, here's the reality: you're the one who ultimately decides how your company manages risk. That includes cyber risk.

When clients lose trust, when regulators come knocking, or when the board demands answers, they're not going to ask what antivirus you use. They'll want to know what leadership did to prevent the breach.

5 Questions the Board Might Ask You After a Breach

(And Why You Should Have Answers *Before* It Happens)

1. **"Did we have an incident response plan, and was it followed?"** They'll want to know if there was a clear process in place, not just a scramble.

2. **"Were we meeting the minimum requirements of our cyber insurance policy?"** Many claims are denied due to the oversight of security controls. This can lead to finger-pointing or, worse, personal liability.

3. **"When was the last time we tested our backups or ran a security drill?** If the answer is "never" or "I'm not sure," expect some tense moments.

4. **"What steps had leadership taken to ensure cybersecurity was a priority?** They're not asking your MSP. They're asking *you*.

5. **"What are we doing to make sure this doesn't happen again?"** The future matters as much as the failure. Boards want reassurance that lessons are being turned into action.

Why this matter to you, not just to your IT team:

Cybersecurity is a business continuity issue.

Just like you prepare for fires, floods, or audits, you need a plan for cyber events. Downtime doesn't just hurt systems; it kills deals, delays payroll, and damages your reputation.

You're accountable, even if you didn't click the link.

Regulators and cyber insurers now expect CEOs to understand their company's security posture. Saying "I didn't know" won't shield you from consequences.

Your example sets the tone.

If your team treats cybersecurity as someone else's job, it's often because leadership is doing the same. Your attitude, good or bad, shapes the culture.

A single breach, especially one that exposes client or patient data, can lead to public backlash, broken contracts, and media attention. You can recover, but rebuilding trust takes time.

That doesn't mean learning to read threat reports. It means:

- Asking the right questions
- Pushing for clear answers from vendors and IT
- Treating cybersecurity as a leadership issue

Think of it like legal or financial risk. You may not do the work yourself, but you make sure it gets done, and you understand the cost of getting it wrong.

Just like legal or financial oversight, cybersecurity has both strategic and technical sides. Your IT lead may configure the defenses, but you're still the one who answers customers, insurers, and regulators. Here's how the responsibilities are usually split:

CEO vs. CIO Responsibilities in Security

Responsibility Area	CEO's Role	CIO's Role
Setting Security Priorities	Sets the tone from the top. Approves budget.	Translates strategy into operational plans.
Risk Oversight	Owns business risk, including cyber risk.	Identifies technical vulnerabilities and solutions.
Board & Client Communication	Represents the company during a crisis.	Provides technical clarity and incident details.
Culture & Accountability	Models secure behavior. Makes security a company value.	Reinforces policies through IT processes.
Incident Response Readiness	Ensures there's a tested plan in place.	Maintains the plan and leads the technical response.
Cyber Insurance Alignment	Ensures the company meets policy requirements.	Helps implement required controls.

CEO Action Checklist: Own the Risk Before It Owns You

Use this list to start taking ownership of your company's cybersecurity posture. You don't need to have all the answers, but you do need to start asking the right questions.

Leadership & Responsibility

- Ask yourself: *If we were hit with ransomware tomorrow, what would I do first?*
- Make it clear to your team that cybersecurity is a leadership priority, not just an IT issue.

Questions to Ask Your IT Team or MSP

- "What would we do if we got hit with ransomware today?"
- "Are we regularly backing up critical data, and are those backups tested?"
- "Can we detect if someone logs in with a stolen password?"
- "Do we have cyber insurance, and do we meet the policy's security requirements?"
- "Who owns our incident response plan, and when was it last tested?"

Business Process Review

- Review your company's cyber insurance policy and coverage

limits.

- Ensure that cybersecurity risk is included on your leadership meeting agenda at least quarterly.
- Confirm that MFA (Multifactor Authentication) is enabled for all systems, particularly email, file storage, and financial tools.

Next Step

- Book time with your IT lead or MSP for a 30-minute cybersecurity briefing.

Use this book to guide the conversation, highlight risks, review responsibilities, and define action items.

Chapter 2

What Hackers Want from Small Businesses

On a quiet Tuesday morning, the CFO of a 60-person financial services firm opened an email that appeared to be from their CEO. The message was short and urgent:

"Are you available to wire a payment to a new vendor this morning? I'll send you the invoice."

The CFO replied, "Yes." A few minutes later, a second email arrived with an invoice and bank details. Everything seemed legitimate: the CEO's name, tone, even the email signature.

By the time they realized it wasn't the CEO, $48,000 had already been spent.

There was no firewall breach. No ransomware. No malware. Just a convincing email and a few minutes of deception.

This is how modern cybercrime works. And it works well, especially against small and midsize businesses.

You might wonder, *Why would hackers care about my company? We're not a bank. We don't store millions of credit card numbers.*

That mindset is precisely what makes small businesses such easy targets.

That $48,000 wire transfer wasn't a rare case. It's part of a broader tactic called Business Email Compromise (BEC), one of the most profitable types of cyberattacks aimed at companies like yours.

According to the FBI's Internet Crime Report, Business Email Compromise (BEC) scams resulted in more than $2.7 billion in losses in just one year, surpassing the combined losses from ransomware and data breaches.

Why do hackers use it? Because it's simple. And it works.

They don't need to hack your systems or plant malware. They need to pose as someone you trust, such as a CEO, a vendor, or a client. They often get the information they need from LinkedIn or your company website.

Once the money's transferred, it's nearly impossible to get it back.

But wire fraud is only one tactic. Here's what else attackers are after when they go after small businesses:

- **Quick money** – Ransomware payouts, wire transfers, or stolen credit card data

- **Login credentials** – Email, payroll, or financial accounts, which are resold on dark web marketplaces

- **Sensitive records** – Customer information, legal files, Social Security numbers, medical data

- **Access to your clients or vendors** – Hackers breach your systems, then use your email to attack others
- **Your team's trust** – A phishing email that looks like it came from you can fool even cautious employees

And the truth is, it doesn't take much to make an attack profitable. If someone can steal $50,000 with one email, your 50-person business is just as appealing to them as a company ten times your size.

Hackers Run Businesses, Too, And You're on Their Target List

Cybercrime today operates like a professional, scalable, and profitable business.

The era of lone hackers driven by curiosity or ideology is largely behind us. Today's threat actors operate like startups. They have sales funnels, dashboards to track victims and payouts, and even a customer service team. Many don't write their code. They rent toolkits, buy stolen credentials in bulk, or use Ransomware-as-a-Service platforms where the developers get a cut of every ransom.

And just like any innovative business, these attackers look for:

- **Low overhead** – Small businesses usually have weaker defenses, fewer controls, and minimal cybersecurity training
- **Repeatable success** – If a phishing email or fake invoice works once, it can be reused across hundreds of targets
- **Fast returns** – One employee mistake can bring in tens of

thousands through ransom, fraud, or stolen data resale

In other words, this isn't random. It's efficient.

Attackers don't care how many employees you have. They care how quickly they can profit and whether you're likely to have defenses in place that slow them down.

This is why small and midsize businesses often get hit hardest:

- You're big enough to have valuable data and steady cash flow
- You're small enough not to have a dedicated security team
- And chances are, you don't think you're a target

That's precisely what makes you appealing.

You're not too small to be attacked. You're just small enough to be vulnerable.

Cybercriminals aren't chasing headlines; they're chasing easy wins. They target companies with sufficient funds to be worth pursuing but not enough defenses to stop them.

Now think about what's sitting on your systems right now:

- Customer records
- Financial statements
- Payroll files
- Contracts and legal documents

- Access to vendor and partner emails

To a hacker, that's a gold mine.

And if you're in healthcare, finance, law, or SaaS? You're even more attractive. These industries handle sensitive data, adhere to strict compliance rules, and rely heavily on digital systems to maintain operational efficiency.

Why Your Industry Is a Target

Industry	Why Hackers Target It
Healthcare	Stores protected health information (PHI); heavily regulated; time-sensitive operations.
Finance	Holds financial records, bank access, payroll details, and wire transfer capabilities.
Legal	Access to sensitive case files, contracts, and client PII; often under-secured.
SaaS	Connected to other businesses via APIs, a potential backdoor into larger clients.
Professional Services	Handles client data, contracts, and payroll; trust-based operations make them vulnerable to spoofing.
Education	Stores student/family data; often underfunded security-wise.
Retail/eCommerce	Collects credit cards and shipping data; targeted for fraud and credential stuffing.

From an attacker's perspective:

- You might never report the breach
- You're likely to pay to make it disappear
- You probably don't have someone checking logs full-time
- And you could lead them to bigger targets, your clients, vendors, or investors

This isn't about fear; it's about understanding your risk.

Just like you insure your office, vehicles, or equipment, cybersecurity protects your revenue, reputation, and future. If an attack shuts you down for even a week, how many deals stall? How many clients start to question your reliability?

And more importantly, what would you owe your clients if their data were compromised on your watch?

CEO Action Checklist: Know What Makes You a Target

Don't wait until you're the one calling a cyber insurance hotline. Use this checklist to identify your weak spots now and take steps to protect what hackers are after most.

Understand Your Risk Profile

- Do we store or transmit sensitive data, such as financial, legal, healthcare, or customer information?
- Do we have access to larger companies or vendors through shared

platforms or integrations?

- Are we processing payments, payroll, or wire transfers internally?

Ask Your Team These Questions

- How easy would it be for someone to impersonate me or another executive?
- What's our process for verifying wire transfers or payment requests?
- Are we monitoring for unauthorized logins or unusual activity?
- Are employees trained to spot phishing emails or spoofed messages?

Lock Down the Basics

- Enable multifactor authentication (MFA) for email, finance, and administrative tools.
- Don't allow wire transfers or other sensitive actions based solely on email requests.
- Schedule phishing awareness training for all employees, particularly those with financial or administrative access.

Take Action This Month

- Meet with your finance lead and IT team to review recent wire or ACH activity.
- Run a business email compromise tabletop exercise: *What would*

we do if someone spoofed our CEO?

- Ask your insurance broker if your current policy covers business email compromise (BEC) or social engineering fraud.

What Your Company Is Worth on the Dark Web

Hackers don't need to crash your systems to profit from you. They quietly harvest credentials, personal data, and access points that can be easily sold on dark web marketplaces.

Here's what your company's sensitive information is typically worth to cybercriminals:

Item	Estimated Dark Web Price
Stolen business email credentials	\$10–\$50 per account[1]
Payroll login (ADP, Gusto, etc.)	\$30–\$500 per login[2]
Wire transfer access credentials	\$500–\$2,000+ per account[3]
Full employee PII (SSN, DOB, W-2)	\$30–\$100 per record[4]
PHI (healthcare data)	\$250–\$1,000 per record[5]
Remote desktop credentials (RDP)	\$3–\$1,000 depending on access level[6]
Compromised SaaS admin account	\$300–\$3,000+ per account[7]

Why your data matters to attackers:

- **Access**: Credentials are gateways into your business and your partners.
- **Money**: Payroll and wire-transfer credentials turn directly into cash.
- **Trust**: Stolen identities and client data erode your reputation and relationships.

Small businesses aren't targeted because of who they are but rather **who they connect to**. Your credentials may unlock doors to larger vendors, partners, or clients, magnifying the damage from a single breach.

CEO Insight:

Think of your company as a valuable digital asset. If your employee logins, customer data, or payment systems have value to your business, rest assured they're even more valuable to someone selling them on the dark web.

Chapter 3

The Cost of Doing Nothing

When a 40-person law firm in the Midwest was hit with ransomware, the managing partner didn't panic at first. Their IT vendor had assured them that backups were in place, and the firm had recently added cyber insurance to their policy.

But the reality was far worse.

The backups were corrupted. The insurance provider denied the claim because the firm had never implemented multifactor authentication, something required in the fine print.

By the end of the month, they had:

- Paid a $75,000 ransom to regain access to case files
- Lost two major clients concerned about confidentiality
- Spent nearly $200,000 on legal fees, forensic investigations, and PR crisis management

All from a single phishing email.

The managing partner later admitted, "We knew we should've done more, but it kept getting pushed to the bottom of the list."

That's the cost of doing nothing, not just in dollars but in trust, reputation, and long-term growth.

What Would It Cost You?

(Customize this worksheet to estimate your company's cyber-breach risk.)

Step 1: Calculate Downtime Cost

- Average Daily Revenue: **$**__________
- Estimated Downtime (days): ________ days
- **Downtime Cost** = (Revenue × Days): **$**__________

Step 2: Estimate Direct Recovery Costs

- IT Recovery (consultants, staff overtime, etc.): **$**__________
- Equipment Replacement (new servers, software, etc.): **$**__________
- Legal & Regulatory Fines: **$**__________
- PR & Customer Communications: **$**__________
- **Direct Recovery Costs Total: $**__________

Step 3: Add Long-Term Impact Costs

- Lost Customers/Contracts (Annual): **$**__________
- Increased Cyber Insurance Premiums: **$**__________
- Ongoing Reputation Management: **$**__________
- **Long-Term Impact Total: $**__________

Your Estimated Breach Cost:

Downtime Costs + Direct Costs + Long-Term Costs = $______________

CEO Insight: Even rough numbers help you prioritize cybersecurity investments by clarifying your financial exposure.

SMB Breach Case Studies

1. Professional Services Firm (35 Employees)

A finance and payroll consulting firm fell victim to a phishing email that impersonated the CEO. An employee clicked a link and entered their credentials on a spoofed login page. The attacker used those credentials to access the payroll system and rerouted several direct deposits.

Cost: $97,000 in lost payroll funds.

Impact: The company recovered some funds but spent months rebuilding employee trust. Their cyber insurance claim was partially denied due to the lack of multi-factor authentication.

2. Small Healthcare Provider (20 Employees)

A ransomware attack encrypted both patient records and backups at a multi-location medical billing service. The attackers demanded $75,000 in cryptocurrency to unlock files. The company paid the ransom but was later fined under HIPAA for failing to maintain proper access controls.

Cost: $75,000 ransom + $110,000 in recovery and fines.

Impact: Regulatory scrutiny, patient attrition, and a damaged reputation resulted in projected annual revenue losses exceeding $50,000.

3. Regional Law Firm (50 Employees)

The CFO of a law firm received an email that appeared to be from a known vendor requesting an urgent wire payment. It was a spoofed account. The firm transferred $200,000 before discovering the fraud.

Cost: $200,000 lost via wire fraud.

Impact: The law firm was unable to recover the funds. Their cyber insurance premiums increased by 60%, and they implemented new controls and mandatory security training across the firm.

Note: *These case summaries are anonymized but based on real-world events and patterns commonly documented in cybersecurity industry reports, including those from Verizon, IBM, and the Ponemon Institute. They are* *designed to reflect the kinds of risks small and mid-sized businesses regularly face.*

It's easy to delay cybersecurity investments. Maybe it's not in this quarter's budget. Maybe you think your company is too small to attract sophisticated attacks. Perhaps nothing has gone wrong yet.

But here's the truth:

Inaction isn't neutral. It increases your risk.

And that risk grows over time.

Financial Losses

- Ransom payments are just the beginning. You'll also deal with downtime, data recovery, client churn, legal fees, and potential fines.
- According to IBM's 2023 *Cost of a Data Breach Report*, companies with under 500 employees faced an average breach cost of $2.98 million. Even partial losses can cripple small businesses.

Legal and Regulatory Exposure

- In sectors such as healthcare, legal, or finance, failing to protect data can result in violations of HIPAA, GLBA, or state breach laws.
- Regulators don't care how small your company is. They want to see if you took reasonable steps; doing nothing won't count as a defence.

Client Trust and Reputation

- Clients may forgive a breach. They won't forgive poor leadership.
- Losing one key client due to a breach can cost more than the ransom. And once news spreads, damage control gets harder.

Cyber Insurance Gaps

- Most cyber insurance policies require basic security measures, such as multifactor authentication (MFA), endpoint protection, and employee training.
- According to Coalition Inc.'s 2023 *Cyber Claims Report*, many claims are denied when those controls are missing.
- The National Cybersecurity Alliance reports that in 2018, 43% of U.S. cyberattacks targeted small businesses. By 2023, the number had risen to 71%. That's a clear signal: attackers are focusing on smaller targets more than ever.

Doing nothing doesn't save money. It stores up a more significant expense for later, with interest.

Cyber incidents rarely give a warning. They hit fast, spread quickly, and leave you with two choices: pay now or pay more later.

Running a business means managing endless priorities, sales, hiring, operations, and compliance. It's tempting to treat cybersecurity as something to address later, especially if nothing has gone wrong yet.

But cyber threats don't wait until it's convenient.

You can delay hiring. You can push a product launch. You can't postpone an attack.

Cybersecurity isn't a future task. It's already being tested by attackers today.

The belief that "we're too small," "we haven't had any issues," or "it's not in the budget right now" isn't cautious; it's dangerous. Here's why:

- Every delay increases your vulnerability. Unpatched software, untrained staff, and neglected systems make you a growing target.
- Hackers don't need a motive. They need an opening, and the longer you ignore the gaps, the wider they get.
- Inaction sends a message. Regulators, insurers, and clients see weak cybersecurity as a sign of poor risk management.

And here's the most brutal truth: If you haven't taken even the most basic steps to protect your business, you may have already been breached, and you don't know it yet.

Cyber risk doesn't wait for your decision.

Doing nothing is the decision.

Procrastination Is a Leadership Liability

You may not be the one configuring firewalls or running phishing simulations, but you are the one setting the company's priorities.

If cybersecurity keeps slipping off your agenda, that's not a technical oversight. That's a leadership gap.

Ask yourself:

- Would you wait until after a break-in to install locks on your office?
- Would you skip insurance on a company vehicle because "we haven't crashed yet"?
- Would you ignore financial risk just because "we've always been profitable"?

Of course not. So why treat cyber risk any differently?

Here's what many CEOs overlook:

- Cybersecurity isn't a one-time project, it's an ongoing posture
- The cost of inaction builds quietly and strikes suddenly
- Your IT team can only prioritize what you've empowered them to act on

And remember, clients and partners are paying attention. Many now include cybersecurity checks in their due diligence, insurance paperwork, and contract requirements. If your business can't answer those questions confidently, you could lose out on deals before they even begin.

According to Gartner's *Third-Party Risk Management Benchmarking Report*, an increasing number of organizations are implementing robust vendor vetting processes to evaluate cybersecurity across the entire vendor lifecycle.

You don't have to do everything. But you do need to start something.

Every month without action is a silent bet that nothing bad will happen. That's not a strategy; it's gambling with your business.

CEO Action Checklist: Don't Wait for the Wake-Up Call

You don't need to become a cybersecurity expert; you need to act like the risk is real because it is.

Here's how to start shifting from reactive to proactive today:

Stop Waiting for a Breach

- Block time this quarter to review your cybersecurity posture with your IT lead or MSP
- Identify what's not being done because of budget, bandwidth, or "we've been lucky so far."
- Make cybersecurity a standing topic in your leadership or partner meetings.

Evaluate Risk and Readiness

- Ask: *If we were attacked tomorrow, who would lead the response?*
- Check: *Are our backups working, tested, and stored offsite?*
- Review: *Are We Meeting the Minimum Standards for Our Cyber Insurance P**olicy**?*

Empower Your Team to Act

- Give IT or your MSP apparent authority and budget to close known gaps.

- Ask for a risk snapshot: What's our most significant vulnerability today?
- Confirm basics: MFA, endpoint protection, phishing training, and role-based access.

Take One Step Forward

- Schedule a tabletop incident response drill.
- Review your cyber insurance policy for any OK print requirements.
- Designate a cybersecurity owner in your leadership team or vendor relationship.

Chapter 4

The Most Common Cyber Threats for SMBs

The IT director of a 120-person healthcare billing company couldn't believe what he was seeing. One of the company's support representatives had clicked a link in what appeared to be a Microsoft password reset email.

Within minutes, the attacker had full access to the employee's inbox.

From there, they downloaded sensitive patient billing records, impersonated the rep to request updated bank account details from multiple clients, and used the compromised account to send phishing emails to other staff members.

It took two days to discover the breach. By then, over 6,000 files had been exfiltrated, and several clients had wired payments to fraudulent accounts.

This wasn't a high-tech breach.

It was a phishing email.

One-click, that's all it took.

Cyber threats don't always come in through the front door. Most attacks on small and midsize businesses start with simple, preventable tactics, the kind many companies assume would never work on them.

This chapter breaks down the most common threats SMBs face, how they work, and why they're so effective, especially in organizations without dedicated security staff or formal incident response plans.

These attacks may not make the news, but they always leave a mark.

For small and midsize businesses, a successful attack can mean:

- Disrupted operations
- Compromised client data
- Stolen funds
- Damaged relationships
- Legal and compliance fallout

News headlines often spotlight breaches at large enterprises, but small to medium-sized businesses (SMBs) account for over 60% of ransomware victims (Verizon DBIR, 2024). That's because attackers know you're more likely to:

- Lack of a dedicated cybersecurity team
- Use weak email and identity protections
- Rely on informal, trust-based communication

- Delay patching software and updating systems

The bigger issue? Most of the threats that hit SMBs don't require advanced skills. They're simple, automated, and profitable. One untrained employee or one unpatched system is all it takes.

And once that gap is exploited, the damage spreads fast:

- Phishing leads to stolen credentials
- Credentials lead to system access
- Access leads to ransomware, data theft, or financial fraud

Many leaders underestimate the interconnectedness of these risks. A single email link can trigger a chain reaction that affects vendors, clients, and compliance status.

You don't need to be targeted by a sophisticated nation-state group to suffer a catastrophic breach. Sometimes, it just takes one person to click the wrong link.

Most Attacks Are Simple and Aimed at You

Cyberattacks come in many forms, but those that hit small and mid-sized businesses the hardest tend to fall into a few predictable and highly effective categories.

Here are the top threats you're most likely to face, explained in plain language:

Phishing and Business Email Compromise (BEC)

- Attackers send fake emails that appear to come from vendors, employees, or platforms like Microsoft or DocuSign.
- Their goal is to get someone to click a malicious link or wire money
- These scams work because the emails often look legitimate, especially when they spoof internal addresses or reply to actual threads

Ransomware

- Malicious software encrypts your files and demands payment to unlock them
- The attacker's goal is to force a ransom payment, often in cryptocurrency
- These attacks succeed when backups are missing, infected, or untested and when downtime is more expensive than paying up

Credential Theft and Account Takeover

- Hackers use stolen usernames and passwords to gain unauthorized access to your systems, email accounts, or cloud applications.
- Once inside, they can access data, impersonate staff, or move deeper into your network.
- These attacks often succeed because people reuse passwords, skip

multifactor authentication, or fall for phishing emails.

Unpatched Software and Vulnerable Systems

- Attackers constantly scan the internet, searching for outdated software, routers, firewalls, or plugins with known vulnerabilities.
- Their goal is to exploit these weaknesses to break in
- This works because many SMBs delay updates or don't know where all their risks are

Insider Threats (Intentional or Accidental)

- A disgruntled employee or careless contractor mishandles sensitive data or turns off security features.
- Sometimes, it's theft; sometimes sabotage; often, just negligence.
- These incidents happen when companies lack role-based access or fail to monitor for unusual activity.

Threat Matrix: Likelihood vs. Business Impact

	High Impact	**Low Impact**
High Likelihood	Phishing / Business Email Compromise (BEC) Credential Theft Unpatched Software	Basic Malware Infections
Low Likelihood	Ransomware (targeted or widespread) Insider Threats (malicious or negligent)	Physical Device Theft Website Defacement

Interpretation Tip for CEOs: Focus most of your energy on threats in the **top-left quadrant**. They happen often and hurt the most. These are where low-effort improvements deliver high returns.

These threats aren't rare. They happen every day. Most are automated, inexpensive to launch, and designed to blend in. Chances are, your company is already receiving dozens, if not hundreds, of these attempts every week.

The good news? You can block most of them with visionary leadership, basic protections, and a few targeted questions.

You Don't Need to Be an Expert, Just Accountable

You don't need to become a cybersecurity expert to lead a secure company. But you do need to understand this:

Most threats that hit small businesses are simple, preventable, and succeed only because of inaction or oversight.

Your job isn't to understand every detail of ransomware. Your job is to:

- Make sure the proper protections are in place
- Set a culture where security is a shared responsibility
- Hold your IT team or service provider accountable for doing the basics

Here's where many CEOs slip up:

- Assuming the MSP or IT team has it all under control, without needing to ask for details.

- Thinking that small businesses are invisible to attackers.
- Believing cybersecurity is mostly about buying expensive tools.

But cybersecurity often comes down to decisions at the leadership level:

- Have you required phishing training for all staff?
- Do your financial and payroll systems use multifactor authentication?
- Have you reviewed your backup, endpoint, and email protections with your team?

When a threat becomes a breach, it won't matter whether it originated from a phishing email or an unpatched server. What matters is whether your company was prepared, and that responsibility begins with you.

Free or Low-Cost Defenses for Each Major Threat

Phishing & BEC

- Simulated phishing emails (e.g., KnowBe4 free tool).
- Email banners for external senders.
- Company-wide "pause before payment" policies.

Ransomware

- Regular backups are stored **either offline or in a cloud service with versioning capabilities**.

- Disable macros in Office files by default.
- Practice a 10-minute tabletop drill: "What would we do right now?"

Credential Theft

- Require MFA on email, payroll, and admin tools (many providers offer it free).
- Use a password manager like Bitwarden (free tier available).
- Educate staff: never reuse work passwords on other sites.

Unpatched Systems

- Turn on **automatic updates** where available.
- Use basic vulnerability scanners (e.g., OpenVAS or Microsoft Defender Recommendations)
- Assign someone monthly to check for software/plugin updates.

Insider Threats

- Role-based access (limit who can see what)
- Exit checklist: remove accounts immediately when someone leaves
- Culture of transparency: mistakes should be reported, not hidden

CEO Action Checklist: Know the Threats, Lead the Defense

You don't need to memorize every attack type, but you **do** need to make sure your business is protected against the most common ones.

Here's what to do this quarter:

Understand Your Exposure

- Ask your IT team or MSP: *"What are the top 3 threats most likely to affect us?"*
- Review recent phishing attempts or spoofed emails with your help desk or security contact.
- Get a list of all third-party systems (email, payroll, CRM) and confirm that MFA is enabled.

Lock Down the Basics

- Confirm that all company email accounts have multifactor authentication (MFA)
- Implement a policy: *No financial or payroll changes will be made via email without prior phone verification.*
- Ensure all employees complete phishing awareness training at least once a year (preferably quarterly)

Ask About These Protections

- Are all software and systems being regularly updated and patched?

- Do we have endpoint protection (antivirus, EDR, or MDR) on every laptop, server, and work-from-home device?
- Are our **backups tested** and stored off-network in the event of a ransomware attack?
- Talk about cybersecurity during an upcoming all-hands or team meeting.
- Include security updates in your executive dashboard or quarterly reporting.

Reinforce the message: **"Security is everyone's job, starting with me."**

Chapter 5

Humans Are the Weakest Link

It wasn't a hacker. It wasn't malware. It was a distracted employee.

An office manager at a 30-person real estate company received what appeared to be an urgent DocuSign email requesting a signature on a closing document. She was multitasking. She clicked. She logged in.

But it wasn't DocuSign. And the login page wasn't actual.

Within an hour, the attacker had full access to her inbox, including sensitive financial information and wire instructions for a $1.2 million transaction. The attacker sent a fake closing document with the client's new bank details. The client wired the money.

By the time anyone realized, the money was gone.

There were firewalls. Antivirus software. Backups. Multifactor authentication is required on most accounts.

None of it mattered because the breach started with a person just trying to do their job.

This chapter examines why people, rather than technology, are the most significant vulnerability in most small businesses and what CEOs can do to mitigate that risk without slowing down the team.

No matter how much you invest in cybersecurity, firewalls, antivirus, email filters, or backups, it only takes one person to undo it all with a single click.

Human error is the leading cause of breaches in small and midsize businesses.

Not hackers breaking in but employees letting them in.

Fictional Email & Response Timeline

Context:
A 60-person marketing agency. The attacker impersonates the CEO.

Phishing Email Transcript

From: ceo@agency-inc.fake [spoofed]
To: accounts@agency-inc.com
Subject: URGENT: Wire Transfer Before Noon
Body:
"Hey, can you send $48,320 to the new vendor we talked about for the web redesign? Use the updated banking info attached. We're onboarding them today. I'm in back-to-back meetings. Let me know once it's done."
Mark

Response Timeline

Time	Event
9:16 AM	Email received by Accounts Payable
9:20 AM	AP clerk replies: "Got it, working on it now."
9:29 AM	Funds are wired to the attacker's offshore account.
11:02 AM	A real CEO responds to an unrelated thread, and AP realizes something's wrong.
11:17 AM	Internal IT confirms the spoofed address.
11:55 AM	The bank was contacted, but the funds are unrecoverable.
3:00 PM	Leadership notifies insurance and legal.

CEO Insight: This doesn't involve sophisticated malware. It's about trust, speed, and pressure. It took less than 30 minutes for one email to cost nearly $50,000.

According to the 2023 Verizon Data Breach Investigations Report:

- 74% of breaches involved human factors like error, misuse, or social engineering
- Phishing remains the most common way attackers gain access,

especially where training is rare

- Stolen credentials are the top prize for attackers, and employees often hand them over unknowingly

Once attackers get in, the damage happens fast:

- Wire fraud and financial losses
- Theft of client data and regulatory consequences
- Damage to trust and reputation
- Internal confusion and lost productivity during cleanup

Most incidents don't come from malicious insiders. They happen because good people make honest mistakes, clicking too quickly, trusting an email sender, or skipping a check under pressure.

You can patch software. You can't fix human behavior.

However, you can cultivate a culture that encourages people to make better choices.

Cybersecurity Isn't Just Technical. It's Behavioral.

When CEOs consider cybersecurity, they often focus on tools, including firewalls, antivirus software, and encryption. But those tools are only as strong as the people using them.

Your employees are both your first line of defense and your most significant point of risk.

Attackers know this. That's why they rely on social engineering. They don't need to break in if they can convince someone to open the door.

Here's how it plays out in most small and midsize businesses:

- Phishing emails that look like Microsoft, DocuSign, or messages from internal staff
- Fake invoices sent to accounts payable teams during busy periods
- "CEO fraud," where attackers impersonate executives to request urgent wire transfers
- Passwords are reused across systems, often without multifactor authentication
- Personal email credentials used to access work systems

These aren't technology problems. They're decision problems. And they happen under stress, distraction, or misplaced trust.

Security awareness training alone won't solve this problem. Watching a 10-minute video once a year won't change behavior. What people need is:

- Repetition
- Real-life context
- Permission to slow down and double-check
- Support from leadership when they raise a concern

That's where you come in, not to write policies but to set the tone. When leaders prioritize security as part of everyday work, not as an afterthought, people follow.

Culture Is Your Best Defense

You can't control every click, every email, or every password.

However, you can control the culture in which your team operates.

When employees feel rushed, unsupported, or afraid of making mistakes, they're more likely to slip up and less likely to speak up when something goes wrong.

That's why protecting your business starts with leadership.

As CEO, your job is to:

- Set the expectation that security is everyone's responsibility, not just IT's
- Create space for people to pause, question, and verify before acting
- Support systems that make secure behavior easy and practical

In real terms, that might look like:

- Requiring verbal confirmation before any wire transfer or payroll change
- Encouraging employees to report suspicious emails, even if they turn out to be harmless

- Publicly recognizing team members who spot and stop phishing attempts
- Make it clear that security isn't a checklist item; it's a core part of how the business runs

If your people are your most significant risk, they can also be your greatest strength.

It all comes down to how you lead.

CEO Action Checklist: Make Security Part of the Culture

People make mistakes. Your job is to lead a culture where those mistakes are caught early and avoided when possible.

Build Awareness and Habits

- Require phishing training for all employees (and repeat it quarterly)
- Ask IT to run simulated phishing tests and report on click rates.
- Encourage employees to report suspicious emails without fear of blame.

Improve Processes

- Enforce MFA on all email, payroll, and admin accounts.
- Require verbal or secondary approval for wire transfers or sensitive changes.

- Ensure employees don't share logins or reuse passwords.

Lead the Way

- Mention cybersecurity in company meetings and emails to ensure a consistent approach to security.
- Celebrate "near misses" to show reporting is valued.
- Set the tone: Security is how we do business, not an afterthought.

Mini Training Guide, How to Spot a Phish

Use this 15-minute checklist at your next team meeting. It's fast, non-technical, and could save your business.

5 Red Flags in a Suspicious Email

1. **Urgency or pressure:** "Send this ASAP" or "Need this before noon."
2. **Unusual requests:** Wire transfers, gift cards, or password resets
3. **Generic greetings:** "Hi, team": instead of your name or title
4. **Spelling or formatting issues**Slight errors that feel off but not obvious
5. **Unfamiliar sender or domain:** The email looks right but isn't quite

3 Things to Teach Your Team

- **Pause** before acting on anything urgent or financial in nature.
- **Verify** the request through a known, separate channel (like Slack or phone)
- **Report** the email to IT or your MSP, even if you're not sure.

CEO Tip: Make it safe to report "false alarms." If your team's afraid of getting it wrong, they'll stay quiet when it matters.

Chapter 6

Why Single Sign-On (SSO) Matters More Than You Think

On a Monday morning, the CEO of a 50-person marketing firm received an alarming call. A client had just been emailed from one of the company's online project accounts. The email originated from an employee who had left the company months prior. How was that possible? It turned out the former staffer's account on a cloud service hadn't been disabled during offboarding. With logins managed separately for each app, a few accounts slipped through the cracks.

That oversight resulted in a sensitive client file being compromised, leading to a significant loss of trust. Sound far-fetched? Unfortunately, it's not. Roughly 83% of ex-employees can still access company systems or data of an employer they no longer work for.

Even tech giants aren't immune. In 2018, Cisco suffered a major incident when a former employee, five months after departure, accessed

Cisco's cloud and deleted critical WebEx data, knocking out services for thousands.

Incidents like these often don't involve elite hackers. They stem from mismanaged logins and password sprawl. With the average business employee juggling 191 passwords across various apps, people inevitably reuse or mishandle them. It only takes one weak or stolen password to wreak havoc. Stolen credentials are responsible for up to 80% of breaches. And consider how many logins fly under the radar: cloud services that employees sign up for without IT's knowledge, so-called shadow IT.

Nearly 80% of employees admit to using unapproved SaaS apps for work. Each of those unmanaged accounts is a potential open door. This chapter introduces a solution to these problems: Single Sign-On (SSO).

In plain English, SSO means employees log in once to a trusted system and gain access to all their cloud services through that one secure account. It's more than just a convenience; it's a way to regain control over scattered passwords and accounts, dramatically reducing business risk. Let's break down what's at stake and why SSO has become a must-have for smart CEOs.

What's at Stake

Shadow IT → Shadow Risk

Today's teams move fast. Employees often sign up for new tools, design platforms, document editors, and collaboration apps without involving IT. This creates a sprawling, invisible web of logins, accounts, and data scattered across systems that no one officially manages.

The problem? You can't secure what you don't know exists.

According to Gartner, shadow IT can account for 30% to 50% of IT spending in some organizations, and each unsanctioned app introduces its access, data, and compliance risks (Wikipedia: Shadow IT). Even if your team isn't acting maliciously, every unsupervised login widens the door for attackers.

The Cost of Manual Offboarding

Think of your offboarding checklist: collect the laptop, restrict email access, and shut down app access. Easy enough, in theory. But in practice, missed accounts are common. A 2023 survey by Beyond Identity found that 83% of employees retain access to at least one system after leaving their job, and 56% reported having used it (Beyond Identity, 2023).

These aren't hypothetical risks. Former employees with lingering access have caused data leaks, sabotage, and even full-blown outages, as seen in Cisco's 2018 WebEx incident, where an ex-employee deleted hundreds of virtual machines five months after leaving the company.

Every missed account is a liability. One old login can lead to one very expensive mess.

Credential Chaos Leads to Breaches

Passwords are still the front door to your business, and they're alarmingly easy to break.

- According to the 2023 Verizon Data Breach Investigations Report, 74% of breaches involve the human element, and 49%

involve stolen credentials (Verizon 2023).

- The average employee manages 191 passwords across work and personal apps, according to LastPass (Lastpass 2024).
- Unsurprisingly, password reuse is rampant. IBM found that 53% of users reuse passwords across multiple accounts, including work and personal systems (IBM 2023).

This chaos creates significant enterprise risk. If one password is compromised, every connected account becomes vulnerable. That's how attackers move laterally, jumping from a low-risk tool, such as a project board, to high-value targets like file storage or financial systems.

Bottom line: You can't afford to manage access to one password at a time. The longer you wait to centralize control, the more blind spots and breach paths you leave open. The real risk isn't high-tech hacking. It's low-tech oversights in access and identity management.

What Is SSO and How Does It Work?

If you've ever wished there were a simpler way to manage all your company's logins without relying on memory, spreadsheets, or luck, Single Sign-On (SSO) is your answer.

One Login to Rule Them All

Single Sign-On means your team logs in once to a trusted identity provider, such as Microsoft Entra ID (formerly Azure AD) or Okta, and from there, gains secure access to all approved apps, including email, CRM, file sharing, accounting, and more.

Behind the scenes, SSO acts like a secure digital passport. It authenticates the user once and then automatically handles login to any connected system without requiring the re-entry of passwords. Instead of managing 191 different credentials, a user only needs one.

Why It Matters

SSO isn't just about convenience. It dramatically improves security and control:

- IT teams can automatically enforce multi-factor authentication (MFA), device rules, and session timeouts across all applications.
- If someone leaves the company, you deactivate one account to cut off access to everything.
- You gain visibility into which apps are in use and where risk might be hiding.

In short, it centralizes identity and access, reduces human error, and gives your team one less thing to forget (or screw up).

Without SSO vs. With SSO

	Without SSO	With SSO
Offboarding Risk	High – manual, error-prone	Low – one account to disable
Password Fatigue	Dozens of passwords per user	One password per user
Shadow IT Visibility	Low – IT doesn't know what's being used	High – apps are registered, and access is visible
MFA Enforcement	Inconsistent or app-by-app	Centralized and mandatory across all apps

Why It Matters to You

SSO isn't just an IT upgrade; it's a business decision that pays dividends in security, efficiency, and peace of mind. Here's what that looks like from the CEO's chair:

Eliminate Offboarding Guesswork

When someone leaves your company, you shouldn't be crossing your fingers hoping every account was shut down. SSO provides a single point of control; with one click, access to all connected systems is revoked. No missed accounts. No surprises.

Simplify Audits and Compliance

Need to prove who had access to what? SSO makes it easy. You get a clean, centralized access log, perfect for satisfying SOC 2, HIPAA, or insurance requirements without the scramble.

Boost Productivity and Cut Costs

When your team only has one login to remember, they spend less time resetting passwords and more time getting work done. Your helpdesk thanks you. So does your bottom line.

Improve Your Insurance Standing

Insurers are increasingly expecting centralized access control for high-risk systems. Having SSO in place helps demonstrate that you're managing access responsibly, which can reduce premiums or prevent payout denials.

SSO isn't just IT hygiene. It's business risk reduction, plain and simple.

This is a low-friction, high-ROI investment that strengthens your cybersecurity posture, simplifies IT management, and gives you more confidence in your team's access control.

CEO Action Checklists: Regain Control with SSO

You don't need to be a security expert to manage access risks. Use this checklist to guide the conversation with your team or provider:

- **Ask your IT team or MSP:** "Do we have SSO in place for our apps?" If not, what would it take to achieve this?

- **Identify your Identity Provider:** Common options include

Microsoft Entra ID, Okta, or Google Workspace. Confirm which one you're using.

- **Prioritize Key Systems:** Start by securing your highest-risk platforms, especially:
  - Finance tools (e.g., QuickBooks, NetSuite)
  - HR platforms (e.g., Gusto, BambooHR)
  - File sharing (e.g., Dropbox, OneDrive, Google Drive)
  - Client-facing tools (e.g., CRMs, ticketing systems)
- **Request a List of Apps That Don't Support SSO:** These outliers often present the greatest risks of offboarding and credential theft. Flag them for review or replacement.
- **Make SSO a Requirement for All New Software:** Add this to your procurement checklist: "Does it support SSO with our identity provider?" If not, it doesn't get approved.

Pro Tip: Treat SSO as a minimum access control standard, just like locks on your office doors. If software can't support it, it shouldn't be managing sensitive data.

Choosing the Right SSO Provider

You don't need to evaluate vendors feature-by-feature, but you *do* need to ask the right questions to ensure your SSO solution is secure, scalable, and aligns with your business needs.

Must-Have Criteria	Why-It-Matters
Wide App Support	Works with the tools your team already uses (Google, Zoom, etc.)
MFA Integration	Centralized enforcement of multifactor authentication
Automated Offboarding	One-click restricts access to all linked apps
Audit Logging & Reporting	Easy to show who has access to what during audits
Security Certifications	Look for SOC 2, ISO 27001 – peace of mind for client trust
Scalability & User Management	Grows with your business and handles contractors or guests
Pricing Transparency	Understand user tiers, licensing, and support costs

Popular SSO Providers to Explore:

- Microsoft Entra ID (formerly Azure AD) – ideal if you're a Microsoft 365 shop
- Okta – highly flexible, strong third-party integrations
- Google Workspace SSO – good for simpler needs if you're all-in on Google
- JumpCloud – SMB-friendly, device + identity management

CEO Tip: Ask your MSP or IT team:

"Do we have a centralized way to revoke access across all apps?"

If the answer is no, it's time to make a change.

Offboarding & Access Risk Checklist

Use this checklist to assess your company's ability to secure accounts following the departure of a key employee.

Question	Yes / No
Do we have a *central list* of all apps our employees use?	☐ / ☐
When someone leaves, is there *one place* to restrict all access?	☐ / ☐
Are we using Single Sign-On (SSO) to tie accounts to a central identity?	☐ / ☐
Does our SSO enforce multifactor authentication (MFA)?	☐ / ☐
Do we regularly audit who has access to what systems?	☐ / ☐
Can we produce a report of employee access for auditors or insurers?	☐ / ☐
Do we review contractor and vendor access on a regular schedule?	☐ / ☐
Do we log all login activity and review alerts for unusual behavior?	☐ / ☐

CEO Tip: If you checked "No" on more than 2–3 items, your offboarding process may leave doors open, even after an employee leaves the company.

SSO vs. Password Manager: What's the Difference?

These tools both reduce password pain, but they solve different problems:

Feature	Password Manager	Single Sign-On (SSO)
What it does	Stores and auto-fills passwords for multiple accounts	Eliminates the need for separate passwords by centralizing login through one identity
User experience	One master password unlocks stored credentials for many apps	One login gets you access to all SSO-connected apps; no autofill is needed
Security benefit	Encourages stronger, unique passwords	Reduces password use entirely where supported
Best for	Apps that don't support SSO	Apps that support modern identity standards (SAML, OIDC)

Password managers help users **manage complexity**.

SSO helps your business **reduce it entirely**.

Where possible, use **SSO for security-critical and frequently used applications and password managers as a fallback for all other applications**.

Chapter 7

Not All MFA Is Created Equal

Why Phishing-Resistant MFA Matters

It was a typical Tuesday morning when the CEO of a regional law firm got the call. One of their paralegals had clicked a link in an email that appeared to be a Microsoft 365 login page. She entered her credentials and then approved the MFA push that appeared.

Thirty minutes later, the attacker was logged into the firm's email system, reading sensitive correspondence and forwarding financial documents to an external address.

The IT director was shocked: "But she had MFA enabled..."

What happened? The attacker used a phishing kit designed to intercept both the password and the MFA approval. It was simple, fast, and effective, and it bypassed the very defense they thought would stop it.

CISA warns that not all MFA is created equal; methods like text messages or push notifications can still be compromised through phishing. This is why they recommend phishing-resistant multi-factor authentication (MFA), such as FIDO2-based authentication or PIV/CAC cards, for higher-security environments.

What's at Stake

Modern MFA is often touted as a security silver bullet, but attackers have already found its gaps.

MFA Fatigue and Push Bombing

When a user receives a login prompt on their phone, they're trained to approve it. Now imagine getting five, ten, or even twenty notifications in a row while you're in a meeting. You might eventually tap "approve" to make them stop. That's exactly what attackers count on.

This tactic, known as MFA fatigue or push bombing, has been used in high-profile breaches, including the attack on Uber's internal systems. The attacker didn't bypass MFA. They annoyed someone into accepting it.

CEO takeaway: If MFA is easy for your users, it might also be easy for attackers.

Legacy MFA Isn't Bulletproof

Do you think SMS codes or app-based one-time passwords (OTPs) are a secure method? They're better than nothing but still vulnerable to:

- **SIM swapping:** An attacker transfers a user's phone number to their own device and intercepts texted codes.

- **Phishing sites:** Fake login pages that capture both credentials and the MFA code.
- **Man-in-the-middle attacks:** Sophisticated setups that intercept login details in real-time.

Even "good enough" MFA isn't good enough anymore, not when automated tools are freely available to bypass it.

Insurance and Compliance Pressure

Cyber insurers are paying close attention to your authentication controls. Some now *require* phishing-resistant multi-factor authentication (MFA) for high-risk accounts, such as admin panels, remote access tools, or financial systems.

Regulators are also tightening their expectations. In 2022, the **Cybersecurity and Infrastructure Security Agency (CISA)** issued clear guidance:

"Implement phishing-resistant MFA wherever possible, especially for high-value targets."

If your MFA setup doesn't meet modern standards, your insurance claims could be denied, and your compliance status may be at risk.

The 2023 Verizon Data Breach Investigations Report found:

- **74%** of breaches involve the human element

- **61%** involve *stolen credentials, specifically*

That means more than half of today's breaches *start with a login*. Phishing-resistant MFA doesn't just protect credentials; it neutralizes them as a weak point altogether.

What Is Phishing-Resistant MFA?

Most business leaders know that multifactor authentication (MFA) is essential. However, not all MFA methods are created equal, and modern phishing attacks can still bypass some of the most common ones.

Phishing-resistant MFA refers to a new class of login security methods that fake websites, intercepted codes, or approval fatigue can't trick. These methods are based on cryptographic keys that verify not just the user's identity but also that they're logging into the *right* site.

What Makes It Different?

Traditional MFA methods (like SMS codes, app-generated codes, and simple push approvals) are vulnerable. Here's why:

- **Users can be tricked** into entering a code on a fake site.

- **Push bombing** tactics overwhelm users with login approvals until they click "Allow" just to stop the noise.

- **SIM-swapping** attacks let hackers intercept SMS codes.

Phishing-resistant MFA stops those tricks cold.

It Uses Cryptography, Not Trust

Instead of asking the user to type in a code, phishing-resistant multi-factor authentication (MFA) methods use **cryptographic key pairs**. These keys are stored in a secure chip (like a hardware token or biometric-enabled device) and validate both:

1. That the user is who they say they are, and
2. They're logging in to a legitimate site, not a fake one.

Examples of Phishing-Resistant MFA

- **FIDO2 Security Keys** – Small physical devices that plug into a USB port or use NFC.
- **Smartcards / CAC / PIV Cards** – Common in government or regulated industries.
- **Platform Authenticators** – Devices like modern iPhones or laptops with biometric login tied to FIDO standards.
- **Push Notifications with Challenge Codes** – Some platforms now offer push alerts that display a code the user must match with what's shown on their login screen, making it much harder to approve a spoofed attempt... but not impossible.

MFA Methods Ranked by Security

Method	Security	Phishing-Resistant?
SMS Codes	Low	✗
Authenticator App (TOTP)	Medium	✗
Basic Push Notification	Medium	✗
Push with Challenge Code Matching	Medium-High	✓ *
FIDO2 Security Key	High	✓
Smartcard (PIV/CAC)	High	✓

*Some challenge-based push methods offer partial phishing resistance, depending on implementation.

Most MFA can still be tricked. Phishing-resistant MFA can't because it confirms what you're logging into, not just who you're. It's the difference between handing over your ID to a security guard... or shouting your password in a crowded room.

Why This Matters to You

You already know MFA is important, but here's the problem: **attackers know it, too.** And many of them have adapted. Today's phishing kits are designed to bypass the outdated multi-factor authentication (MFA) methods that most small and mid-sized businesses rely on.

That means using basic MFA (like SMS codes or tap-to-approve push notifications) can give you a **false sense of security** and leave you just as vulnerable as before.

Why Phishing-Resistant MFA Should Be On Your Radar:

Attackers Have Evolved, So Must You

The easy tricks still work. Fake login pages, push bombing, and intercepted codes are cheap, scalable, and shockingly effective. If your business is still using old-school MFA, you're defending against last year's threat, not today's.

Every FIDO Login Is One Less Risk

You don't need a 100% rollout to get value. Every critical login protected by phishing-resistant multi-factor authentication (MFA) reduces your attack surface and improves your odds of avoiding a breach. It's targeted protection with high impact.

It's Not Just a Tech Thing Anymore, It's an Audit Thing

Modern MFA isn't just a best practice; it's increasingly an expectation. **Cyber insurers**, auditors, and regulators are starting to ask:

"Are you using phishing-resistant MFA for your most sensitive systems?"

Being able to say yes:

- Improves your insurability

- Reduces your audit pain
- Lowers your compliance burden

Start with the Crown Jewels

You don't need to roll this out company-wide overnight. Start where the risk is highest:

- Executive logins
- Financial systems
- HR or payroll platforms
- Admin consoles for your cloud apps

Then, it expands over time as adoption grows.

CEO Action Checklist: Raise the Bar on Login Security

You don't need to become a cybersecurity expert to make smarter authentication decisions. Use this checklist to guide your leadership team toward stronger, phishing-resistant multi-factor authentication (MFA).

Ask the Right Question

"Are we using phishing-resistant MFA anywhere in our environment?"

This one question can reveal whether your team is still relying on outdated, vulnerable methods, such as SMS codes or basic push notifications.

Identify High-Risk Roles

Focus first on roles with access to sensitive data or systems:

- Finance and payroll
- Legal and HR
- IT administrators
- C-suite executive accounts
- Cloud app admin portals

Pilot with a Small Group

Select a handful of key users to test security keys, such as YubiKeys or Google Titan Keys.

Start small. Learn fast. Expand smartly.

Add to Your Insurance Checklist

Some cybersecurity insurers now ask about MFA specifics.

Make sure "phishing-resistant MFA for critical systems" is part of your readiness checklist.

Raise the Bar for Vendors Too

Require phishing-resistant multi-factor authentication (MFA) for any new vendors or partners with privileged access to your systems or data.

This helps close gaps that attackers can exploit through the supply chain.

Disable Less Secure MFA Methods

Once you've piloted phishing-resistant MFA and know it works for key roles, start phasing out weaker methods, especially for sensitive systems.

- Disable SMS codes for admin, finance, or cloud logins
- Turn off email-based verification where possible
- Avoid push notifications that don't require user interaction or context

These legacy options are better than nothing but worse than what is now available. By keeping them around, you're creating a false sense of security for your team and an easy opportunity for attackers to exploit.

Ask your IT team, "Where are we still allowing SMS or app codes for logins, and why?"

"But Our Staff Hates MFA"

You'll hear it every time you raise the bar on login security:
"It's annoying."
"I forgot my phone."
"Why do I have to do this again?"
These frustrations are real, but they don't outweigh the risks. A little friction today is better than a six-figure breach tomorrow.

Better Options = Fewer Complaints

Not all MFA is created equal, and not all of it is painful. Here's how to make secure logins easier (and more likely to stick):

- **Use Device-Based FIDO Keys:** Security keys, such as YubiKeys or Google Titan Keys, can be kept on a keychain or plugged into laptops. They're fast, phishing-resistant, and don't rely on a phone.

- **Leverage Built-In Biometric Tools:** Many modern laptops and phones now support FIDO2 authentication via fingerprint or facial recognition, eliminating the need for extra hardware.

- **Skip the Code Copy-Paste:** Users don't need to juggle text messages or authenticator apps when phishing-resistant multi-factor authentication (MFA) is in place. It's faster than older MFA once deployed.

CEO Tip: Resistance to change is a normal response. Focus on ease of use, lead by example, and remind your team one extra click could save the company.

Chapter 8

5 Questions Every CEO Should Ask Their IT Team

The CEO of a 90-person financial advisory firm sat across from a forensic investigator, reading through a breach report.

Attackers had been inside the company's systems for over two months, quietly gathering data from emails, shared drives, and CRM notes. The breach only came to light after a client flagged a suspicious email that included confidential portfolio details to which no one outside the firm should have had access.

The CEO asked, "How did this happen?"

The investigator's reply:

"No one was watching. You didn't have logging turned on, and there were no alerts to detect unusual access."

That CEO had assumed their managed service provider had it all covered. They didn't ask the hard questions because they didn't know what to ask.

This chapter is here to change that.

You don't need to be a technical expert. However, you need to ask the right questions to determine whether your business is genuinely protected or merely hoping that nothing goes wrong.

Many CEOs assume cybersecurity is handled once they've hired an MSP or assigned someone to manage IT. But in security, assumptions are dangerous. If you're not asking the right questions, you won't see the gaps until it's too late.

Here's what's really at stake:

Blind Spots

Without asking the right questions, you might be:

- Backing up data to a location that's never been tested
- Allowing employees to access sensitive systems without MFA
- Logging nothing, detecting nothing, and assuming all is well

Costly Breaches

When those blind spots go unnoticed, attackers take advantage:

- Ransomware locks you out of your data
- Phishing leads to wire fraud or stolen credentials
- Data leaks trigger legal trouble and deny insurance claims

Reputation and Client Loss

Clients expect you to protect their data. If you can't explain what happened or how you discovered it, trust erodes quickly.

Cyber Insurance Risk

More insurers now require proof of controls, such as endpoint protection, offsite backups, and multifactor authentication (MFA). If you can't confirm these are active, you may lose coverage when you need it most.

Not asking questions doesn't reduce your risk; it increases it.

The good news is that you don't need technical skills, just the proper conversation.

You Need to Ask the Right Questions

As CEO, your role isn't to configure firewalls or choose antivirus software.

Your role is to lead, and that starts with asking better questions.

You don't need to become more technical. What you need is visibility.

Asking the right questions:

- Surface weak spots your team might overlook
- Sparks strategic discussions about risk and preparation
- Builds accountability without micromanaging

If you ask nothing, you'll hear, "Everything's fine."

Ask the right things, and you'll uncover what needs attention.

In the next section, we'll cover five essential questions that every CEO should ask their IT team, MSP, or cybersecurity provider regularly.

Each question is designed to:

- Expose blind spots
- Translate risk into business terms
- Help you lead from a position of clarity, not assumption

The Five Questions

Question 1: "How Would We Know If We Were Breached?"

Strong Answer:

"We have centralized logging and get alerts for unusual logins, large data transfers, or failed login attempts. Our MSP monitors these daily, and we review reports weekly."

Weak Answer:

"We have antivirus, and we'd probably notice if something strange happened."

Most breaches aren't discovered right away. They often go unnoticed for weeks or even months and are usually uncovered by a client, vendor, or law enforcement.

So ask:

"If someone broke into our systems today, how would we find out?"

Why this matters:

- Many small and mid-sized businesses lack centralized logging, alert systems, or personnel actively monitoring for suspicious behavior.
- Without detection tools, attackers can operate quietly, stealing data, reading emails, and impersonating staff.

What to listen for:

- Are audit logs enabled for email, file sharing, and administrative accounts?
- Is there a system actively monitoring for unusual activity (like logins from unexpected locations or large file transfers)?
- Who reviews these alerts, and how often?

Follow-up action:

- Ask for a demonstration or report showing how unusual activity is detected.
- If you work with a managed service provider (MSP), ask them directly: *"Have you ever detected a breach for one of your clients? How did you catch it?"*

Question 2: "Are Our Backups Ransomware-Proof and Tested?"

Strong Answer:

"Yes, backups run nightly to a cloud-based, immutable storage system. They're isolated from the network and tested monthly through recovery drills."

Weak Answer:

"We think they're working. We haven't needed to restore anything in a while."

Everyone says they have backups until they need to use them.

So ask:

"Are our backups protected from ransomware, and when were they last tested?"

Why this matters:

- Ransomware often targets backups first, encrypting or deleting them to force payment.
- If your backups reside on the same network as your active data, they can also be vulnerable to compromise.
- A backup that has never been tested isn't a plan; it's a guess.

What to listen for:

- Are your backups stored offsite or in a separate environment?

- Are they immutable or air-gapped, protected from being altered or deleted by ransomware?
- Are test restores done regularly to confirm the backups work?

Follow-up action:

- Ask for proof of the last successful test restore.
- Confirm how long it would take to recover your critical systems.
- If a third party manages your backups, ask for their backup and recovery service-level agreement (SLA).

Question 3: "Do All Critical Systems Require Multifactor Authentication?"

Strong Answer:

"MFA is enforced on email, payroll, financial systems, and admin tools. It's required for all employees and part of our onboarding checklist."

Weak Answer:

"We use MFA on some systems. We've been meaning to roll it out everywhere."

Passwords alone aren't enough. If attackers obtain a password, MFA is often the only thing that stops them from gaining access.

So ask:

"Is multifactor authentication (MFA) turned on for all critical systems, especially email, finance, and admin tools?"

Why this matters:

- Credential theft is the most common method by which attackers gain access.
- MFA blocks over 99% of attacks, even if a password is stolen (Microsoft Blog).
- Email, payroll, banking, and cloud platforms are prime targets for cyberattacks.

What to listen for:

- Is MFA enabled for Microsoft 365, Google Workspace, QuickBooks, NetSuite, banking portals, and admin dashboards?
- Is MFA enforced for the whole company or only for specific users?
- Are there any systems where MFA isn't enabled or not available?

Follow-up action:

- Request a list of systems with and without Multifactor Authentication (MFA).
- If your IT team says, "We're working on it," make it a must-do, not a someday project.
- Inquire about how new users are onboarded and whether multifactor authentication (MFA) is integrated into that process.

Question 4: "Who Has Access to What, and How Often Is That Reviewed?"

Strong Answer:

"Access is based on roles. We review permissions quarterly, especially after role changes or employee exits. No shared accounts are used."

Weak Answer:

"Everyone who needs access has it. We don't have a process for reviewing that."

Most breaches don't involve breaking down digital doors; they involve attackers using access that someone already had and shouldn't have.

"Do we know who has access to our sensitive systems and data, and do we review that access regularly?"

Why this matters:

- Former employees, contractors, or staff who've changed roles often retain access they no longer need
- Shared logins or broad admin privileges are common shortcuts, but dangerous ones
- The more access someone has, the more damage a mistake or breach can cause

What to listen for:

- Is there a clear list of who has access to which systems?

- Is role-based access control (RBAC) in place so users only see what they need?
- How often are access levels reviewed, especially after someone changes roles or leaves the company?

Follow-up action:

- Request an access audit of your most sensitive systems, email, file storage, finance, and HR
- Ask how quickly access is revoked when someone exits the company
- If you use an MSP, ask directly: *"Do you still have admin access to our systems?"*

Question 5: "Do We Have an Incident Response Plan, and Has It Been Tested?"

Strong Answer:

"Yes, our incident response plan covers containment, communication, and recovery. It was last reviewed in Q1 and tested in a tabletop exercise with leadership."

Weak Answer:

"We'd probably call IT and figure it out from there."

No matter how strong your defenses are, you should assume that something will eventually go wrong.

So ask:

"What's our plan if we get hit, and has it been tested recently?"

Why this matters:

- Every minute counts during a cyberattack
- Delays caused by confusion or disorganization only make things worse
- You need a clear plan that outlines who does what, how quickly, and in what order

What to listen for:

- Is there a written incident response plan (IRP)? Has leadership seen it?
- Does the plan cover communication, containment, investigation, and recovery?
- Has it been tested through a tabletop exercise or live drill?

Follow-up action:

- Ask to see the most recent copy of your IRP
- If there isn't one, schedule time with your team or MSP to build it
- Assign roles now, before you're in crisis mode

Asking these five questions isn't about catching your team off guard.

It's about identifying risks before attackers do.

CEO Action Checklist: Ask Better Questions. Get Better Protection.

You don't need to know how to configure a firewall.

You need to lead with the right questions.

Use this list at your next leadership meeting or MSP check-in:

- Schedule a 30-minute review with your IT team or MSP
- Assign ownership of any unclear or unanswered items
- Include this checklist as part of your quarterly executive review

CEO Cybersecurity Scorecard

Use this worksheet to rate how confident you are in your IT team or MSP's answers to the five essential questions.

Question	☑ Strong	! Partial	✕ Weak/Unknown
1. Breach Detection	☐	☐	☐
2. Backups & Testing	☐	☐	☐
3. MFA Everywhere	☐	☐	☐
4. Access Review	☐	☐	☐
5. Incident Response Plan	☐	☐	☐

How to use it:

- 4–5 Strong = You're in solid shape
- 2–3 Partial = Your team may need help or structure
- 0–1 Strong = It's time for a full cybersecurity review

Chapter 9

Building a Culture of Security

At a fast-growing 75-person marketing agency, the CEO felt confident that security was in place. They had a reputable MSP, antivirus on every device, and nightly backups.

Then, a junior account manager clicked on a phishing email.

The attacker used the compromised account to contact clients, request password resets on linked platforms, and steal creative files for an unreleased campaign. The fallout cost them their most significant client, who felt blindsided and betrayed.

The CEO's response?

"We had the tools in place. But our people didn't know what to look for, and no one thought to double-check anything."

That's the difference between having security tools and having a security culture.

You can't train people to be vigilant after something goes wrong.

You need to build awareness and accountability before anything happens.

This chapter examines how CEOs foster such a culture. Not with policies. With leadership.

Tools don't protect your business; your people do.

And when they're not thinking about security, even the best systems can fail. It only takes one missed warning sign, one unverified wire transfer, or one file sent to the wrong place.

Security isn't just a technical problem. It's a people problem.

Without a strong culture of security, your business faces:

- More frequent incidents because employees don't recognize threats
- Slower responses because no one knows who to notify or what to do
- Silent failures because people are afraid to report mistakes
- Damaged client trust because preventable issues keep happening

According to industry reports, the average small business experiences at least one major security incident per year. And in most cases, it's not caused by a failed tool; it's a breakdown in awareness, communication, or accountability.

Worse still, most companies don't realize how weak their security culture is until something goes wrong.

A strong security culture doesn't just help prevent breaches; it also helps protect against them.

It helps your company recover faster when one happens.

Security Culture Is a Leadership-Driven Advantage

Every company has a culture. The question is whether yours makes secure behavior automatic or optional.

A strong security culture isn't built solely on policies. It's about how your team thinks, reacts, and communicates when something feels off. It's about the habits they make, the standards they follow, and the space leadership creates to support responsible action.

If your team sees security as "someone else's job," that's a culture problem.

Here's what a healthy security culture looks like:

- **Awareness** – Employees recognize common threats and know what to look for
- **Communication** – People feel safe reporting mistakes or suspicious activity
- **Reinforcement** – Security is discussed regularly, not just during annual training
- **Accountability** – Expectations are clear, and poor practices are addressed

And here's what a weak one looks like:

- Silence when someone makes a mistake
- Confusion about who to notify when something seems off
- Training that's done once a year, then forgotten
- An attitude of "That's IT's job, not mine."

You don't build a security culture with one policy or a single training session. You achieve this over time through effective leadership, clear communication, and consistent follow-through. That's a key point emphasized in the SANS Security Awareness Maturity Model, which highlights the importance of reinforcement and leadership in managing human risk (SANS Institute, 2023).

Case Study 1 – Success: Culture as a Competitive Edge

Company: SaaS firm with 40 employees

Scenario: A support rep received an email from a customer that "just felt off." Rather than responding, they flagged it. IT confirmed it was a spoofed message trying to gain system access.

Why it worked: The company held monthly security moments in team meetings, and a CEO reinforced that reporting anything suspicious was a success, not a failure.

Outcome: No breach. Leadership rewarded the employee with public praise and a $100 gift card.

Case Study 2 – Failure: Silence After a Mistake

Company: Real estate services company with 25 staff

Scenario: An employee accidentally clicked a phishing link but didn't report it out of fear of getting in trouble. The attacker used their credentials to send malicious attachments to clients.

Why it failed: Security training was rare, and leadership never discussed cybersecurity in meetings. Staff assumed silence was safer than speaking up.

Outcome: A lost client, reputational damage, and a $20,000 remediation cost.

Case Study 3 – Turnaround: Leadership Reset

Company: Multi-location dental group (60 employees)

Scenario: A ransomware incident took down internal systems and exposed poor habits, including reused passwords, unclear reporting processes, and a lack of backup access.

What changed: The CEO took charge. They held a post-mortem, implemented recurring training, and created a "no-blame" culture for reporting security concerns.

Outcome: 1 year later, a phishing attempt was reported in under 5 minutes, allowing the IT team to quarantine the threat before the damage occurred.

Culture Starts with You

Security culture isn't built in IT; it's built in the C-suite.

The NIST Framework also emphasizes that creating a culture of cybersecurity begins with leadership. This involves defining roles, setting clear expectations, and modeling the desired behavior throughout the organization (NIST, 2020).

Employees take their cues from leadership. If you focus on revenue, they'll prioritize growth. If you highlight innovation, they'll focus on creativity. And if you never talk about cybersecurity, they'll assume it doesn't matter.

Your actions as CEO set the tone more than your policies do.

Here's how to lead by example:

- Talk about security during all-hands meetings, not just after an incident
- Recognize and reward employees who report suspicious activity or suggest improvements
- Set clear expectations that security is part of everyone's job, not just IT
- Keep leadership engaged by asking thoughtful questions regularly (see Chapter 6)

The best-performing teams don't treat security as an interruption.

They treat it as part of their standard operating procedure because leadership has made it a priority.

CEO Action Checklist: Lead the Culture, Don't Just Approve the Tools

Security culture starts at the top, and it only sticks if leadership sets the tone.

Use this checklist to shift from reactive to proactive leadership:

Normalize Secure Behavior

- Talk about cybersecurity at least once a quarter in company-wide meetings.
- Reinforce that security is everyone's responsibility, not just IT.
- Ensure phishing simulations and security training are ongoing rather than one-time events.

Make Reporting Easy and Encouraged

- Remove fear: Make it safe for employees to report mistakes or suspicious activity.
- Celebrate security wins: Recognize people who catch phishing attempts or raise concerns.
- Ask your managers: *"If someone on your team got phished, would they tell you?"*

Lead by Example

- Follow the same security policies your team does (MFA, verification steps, device use)

- Ask security questions in leadership meetings.

Demonstrate to your team that security is integral to business success, not a burden.

Checklist: Signs of Weak Security Culture

Use this list to assess whether your company's culture supports cybersecurity or silently works against it.

- People think security is "IT's job," not theirs
- Employees don't report suspicious activity or don't know how
- Mistakes are punished or hidden, not learned from
- Security training happens once a year (or less)
- Phishing simulations are met with confusion or resentment
- Leadership never brings up cybersecurity in meetings
- People share logins or use the same password for multiple tools
- There's no feedback loop for improving processes when issues arise

If you checked 3 or more, your culture may be exposing you to preventable risk.

Chapter 10

Cyber Insurance, Compliance, and Legal Risk

The CEO of a 55-person healthcare staffing agency thought they were covered.

They had cyber insurance, a managed IT provider, and employee compliance training in place. But when a ransomware attack locked down sensitive files, including patient data, their insurance provider refused to pay.

Why? They hadn't enforced multifactor authentication (MFA) across all systems. It was a requirement buried deep in the policy, and no one had flagged it.

To make matters worse, they were later fined under HIPAA for failing to adequately safeguard protected health information. One incident. Two costly hits: an insurance denial and regulatory penalties (HHS, 2023).

As the CEO later said, "We thought compliance meant we were secure. And we thought insurance meant we were protected."

This chapter is about avoiding that exact trap.

Cyber insurance doesn't cover everything, and compliance doesn't guarantee security. But both are crucial for protecting your business from the fallout of a breach.

When a cyberattack occurs, it's not just a technical issue; it's a financial, legal, and reputational crisis.

Too many CEOs assume insurance will bail them out or that being "compliant" means being secure. In reality, both can fail you if you're not paying close attention to the fine print.

Here's what's really on the line:

Cyber Insurance Coverage Denials

- Insurance providers are tightening their requirements
- If you can't prove you had MFA, endpoint protection, or offsite backups in place, your claim may be denied, even if you paid every premium (Coalition, 2023)
- Many policies don't automatically cover social engineering fraud like CEO impersonation or invoice scams unless you've added specific endorsements.

Regulatory Fines and Investigations

- Businesses in regulated industries, including healthcare, finance, and legal, are held to data protection standards under HIPAA,

GLBA, PCI DSS, and similar laws.

- A breach can lead to audits, fines, and required public disclosures
- Most regulations require "reasonable safeguards," and what's considered reasonable keeps evolving

Legal Risk from Clients and Vendors

- Many contracts include clauses about data protection and breach notification.
- Failing to meet those expectations could lead to lawsuits, terminated contracts, or claims of breach (Gartner, 2024)

Reputational Damage

- Even if your insurer pays, your clients may not stay
- Being "compliant" won't matter if the headline says your company lost control of sensitive information

It's not just about whether you get hacked.

It's about how well you've prepared, on paper and in practice, before it happens.

Insurance and Compliance Are Not the Same as Security

Cyber insurance and regulatory compliance are essential, but they're not substitutes for strong cybersecurity practices.

Overlapping, but not equal

	Security Protecting systems, data, and people	**Compliance** Meeting legal & regulatory requirements
Driven by	Risk amangement & best practices	Industry rules & audit checklists
Type	Proactive and evolving	Reactive & document heavy
Enforced by	You & IT / MSP	Regulators, Auditors
Failure Risk	Breaches, Operational Down time	Fines, legal penalties, audit failure

	Cyber Insurance Transferring finanacial risk
Driven by	Policy language and underwriting criteria
Type	Reactive - Triggers only after an incident
Enforced by	Insurers, via claims reviews
Failure Risk	Deined claims, increased recovery costs

Compliance is about meeting minimum standards.

Insurance is about transferring risk.

Security is about protecting your business (NIST, 2022).

Let's break that down:

Compliance

Regulations like HIPAA, PCI DSS, and GDPR define what you must do to operate legally and ethically in your industry. But:

- Compliance tends to be reactive, focused on checklists and documentation

- You can be fully compliant and still vulnerable if your practices are outdated or inconsistently enforced

Cyber Insurance

Cyber insurance helps cover the cost of a breach, but only if:

- You meet the technical requirements spelled out in the policy (often buried in the fine print).
- You've already taken reasonable steps to reduce the risk.

Insurers are raising the bar. Many now require:

- Proof that MFA is enabled on critical systems
- Offsite, tested backups
- Endpoint protection and phishing training
- A documented incident response plan (Insureon, 2025)

If you can't provide evidence, your payout may be denied.

Security Posture

This is what truly protects your business. It includes:

- The tools and controls you implement
- The policies you enforce
- The culture you build (see Chapter 7)

You can't outsource accountability.

When something goes wrong, your clients, partners, and regulators won't be looking at your policy binder. They'll be looking at you.

You're Not Just Buying Coverage, You're Buying Expectations

As CEO, you're not expected to read every clause in an insurance policy or compliance framework. But you are expected to understand what they require from your business.

Both insurance and compliance come with strings attached.

Ignore them, and you risk paying twice: once for the policy and again when it fails to protect you.

Here's what that means for your role:

Cyber Insurance Isn't Set-and-Forget

- Don't assume your broker or IT team has reviewed all the requirements
- Ask: *"What controls are required for our cyber insurance to be valid?"*
- Request documentation that shows you meet those standards, especially MFA, backups, endpoint protection, and training

Cyber Insurance Requirements Checklist

Use this list to review what most insurers now expect from small and midsize businesses. (Requirements vary by policy; ask your broker or provider.)

- **Multifactor Authentication (MFA)**

Enabled on email, remote access, financial systems, and admin tools

- **Offsite and Tested Backups**

Stored in a separate cloud environment or offline, tested at least quarterly

- **Endpoint Protection**

Antivirus and EDR (Endpoint Detection and Response) on all company devices

- **Employee Security Training**

Annual training plus phishing simulations or awareness programs

- **Incident Response Plan**

A documented, tested plan for identifying, containing, and reporting incidents

- **Vendor Risk Management**

Policies for handling third-party vendors with access to sensitive data

- **Email Filtering and Anti-Phishing Controls**

Spam filtering, domain protection (like DMARC), and alerting in place

CEO Tip: Ask your insurance broker: "What could void our policy?" Then, confirm your IT team or MSP can prove those controls are active.

Compliance Doesn't Equal Safety

- Passing an audit doesn't mean your systems are secure
- Focus on day-to-day practices that keep data safe, not just checking boxes
- Work with your legal team or MSP to ensure you meet the spirit of the law, not just the letter

Most Common Cyber Insurance Claim Denials

Reason for Denial	What It Means	How to Avoid It
MFA not enforced on critical systems	You didn't enable MFA on email, cloud apps, or finance tools	Require MFA company-wide; confirm enforcement, not just availability
Backups not tested or insufficiently isolated	Backups were either encrypted by ransomware or failed to restore	Store backups offsite; test quarterly
No documentation of the incident response plan	You lacked a formal response playbook	Create, review, and test an IRP; assign responsibilities
Unpatched vulnerabilities	Outdated software created an easy path in	Apply updates regularly; automate where possible
No proof of employee security training	Training was informal or undocumented	Use training platforms that track completion and offer reports
Social engineering exclusion (not covered)	CEO fraud, wire fraud, or phishing scams weren't part of your coverage	Add social engineering fraud as an endorsement to your policy

CEO Tip: Insurance doesn't just require payment; it requires *proof*. Know what your provider expects **before** something goes wrong.

Your Role Is Oversight

- Make cyber risk a standing topic at board or leadership meetings
- Request quarterly updates on compliance and insurance status
- Clarify who owns what: Who manages policy reviews? Who handles training? Who oversees documentation and claims?

If you rely on third parties, your MSP, IT director, or insurance provider, remember this:

They may share responsibility, but you still own the outcome.

CEO Action Checklist: Protect the Business Beyond the Paperwork

Compliance and insurance matter, but they're not enough on their own. Use this checklist to ensure you're not left exposed.

Cyber Insurance: What to Confirm

- Ask: *"What security controls are required for our policy to pay out?"*
- Verify MFA, backups, endpoint protection, and employee training are in place.
- Request a copy of the most recent cyber insurance policy and have someone review it with you.

Compliance: What to Track

- Know which laws apply to your industry (HIPAA, GLBA, PCI DSS, etc.)
- Assign ownership for compliance reviews and documentation to ensure timely completion and adherence to established guidelines.
- Ensure that security policies are not only written but also enforced.

Oversight: What to Lead

- Bring up insurance and compliance in leadership meetings at least quarterly.
- Ask: *"If we were breached today, would our insurance pay? Would we face fines?"*

Schedule regular updates from your IT team or Managed Service Provider (MSP) on the status of security controls.

Chapter 11

Budgeting for Cybersecurity Without Breaking the Bank

The COO of a 40-person SaaS company asked their IT manager to put together a cybersecurity budget. What came back was a 19-line spreadsheet filled with tools, acronyms, and a five-figure price tag.

The CEO's reaction?

"We're not a bank. Why does it feel like we're budgeting for the Pentagon?"

Frustrated and unsure of what mattered, they delayed most of the spending. Six months later, they were hit with a ransomware attack that shut down client access for three days.

The recovery costs? Nearly four times the original budget.

This chapter is for every CEO who's felt overwhelmed, confused, or burned by cybersecurity costs that seemed more like a black hole than a strategic investment.

The truth is, you don't need a massive budget to significantly reduce your risk. You need to spend the right amount on the right things with a clear plan.

Cybersecurity feels expensive until you experience the cost of doing nothing.

Too often, small and mid-sized businesses either overspend on the wrong tools or underspend entirely due to confusion or sticker shock. Both paths lead to the same place: gaps that leave your business vulnerable (TechTarget, 2022).

Here's what poor budgeting can cost you:

Recovery Costs

- The average company pays $720,000 to recover from a ransomware attack (Coveware, 2023)
- That figure doesn't include downtime, lost revenue, legal fees, or reputation repair.

Wasted Spending

- Buying overlapping tools
- Overpaying for features, no one uses
- Investing in "checkbox" products that don't reduce your

real-world risk

Delayed Investments

- Putting off affordable improvements, like MFA or employee training, that could have prevented a breach

Compliance Penalties and Insurance Gaps

- Failing to invest anything could leave you out of compliance or ineligible for insurance coverage.

Smart cybersecurity budgeting isn't about spending more; it's about spending better.

You can't protect everything. However, you can protect what matters most without blowing your budget if you align your cybersecurity efforts with your actual risks and business priorities.

Cybersecurity Is a Business Investment, Not an IT Expense

Cybersecurity shouldn't be a vague line item buried in your IT budget. It should be treated like any other strategic investment, considering risk, return, and business priorities.

You're not just buying tools.

You're buying protection.

You're buying time.

You're buying trust.

Here's how CEOs should approach cybersecurity spending:

Good Security Is Tiered, Not All-or-Nothing

You don't have to go from zero to enterprise-grade security overnight. Smart security is layered. Small wins add up quickly:

- Start with MFA before jumping into advanced identity platforms
- Provide basic phishing training before running complex simulations
- Use endpoint protection before scaling into complete SOC monitoring

Cybersecurity Sample Budgets

These sample budgets illustrate what smart cybersecurity spending might look like at various scales:

Budget Tier	What You Get	Typical Use Case
$500/month	Basic Endpoint Protection (antivirus/EDR) MFA (email & admin systems) Employee phishing & awareness training (annual)	Small teams (5-20 users), minimal sensitive data
$2,000/month	Advanced endpoint protection with monitoring MFA enforced everywhere Quarterly security training Managed backups & recovery tests	Mid-size teams (20-50 users), moderate sensitive data, growing client base
$10,000/month	Fully Managed Detection & Response (MDR) Service 24×7 Security Operations Center (SOC) monitoring Comprehensive endpoint & server protection Advanced phishing simulations Cybersecurity compliance management	Larger or high-risk SMBs (50-250 users), regulated industries (finance, healthcare, legal, SaaS)

CEO Insight: The key isn't how much you spend; it's whether you're targeting your biggest risks first. Start small, then expand as you grow.

Spend Where the Risk Is Highest

You don't need to protect everything equally. Focus on what matters most:

- Email and identity, where most attacks begin
- Financial systems, where the money lives
- Client data, what regulators and customers care about
- Endpoints, where attacks are executed

Security = Resilience

You're not just trying to prevent every attack. You're investing in your ability to respond and recover. That means budgeting for:

- Fewer incidents
- Faster recovery
- Lower financial impact

You don't need a big budget. You need a clear plan. Start where the risk is most significant. Build from there.

High ROI Cyber Investments for SMBs

These investments deliver significant returns on your cybersecurity dollars, providing maximum risk reduction at minimal cost:

1. **Multifactor Authentication (MFA)**
    - **Why:** Blocks 99% of credential-based attacks (Microsoft

Report, 2023).

- **Cost:** Often free or very low-cost through existing platforms (Office 365, Google Workspace).

2. **Phishing Training & Awareness**
    - **Why:** Reduces human error incidents, which account for over 85% of breaches (Verizon DBIR, 2023).
    - **Cost:** Typically under $10 per user per year for basic annual training.
3. **Endpoint Detection & Response (EDR)**
    - **Why:** Detects and stops threats early, reducing response costs by tens of thousands per incident.
    - **Cost:** Approximately $5-$15 per device per month, depending on features.
4. **Tested Backups (Offsite or Cloud)**
    - **Why:** Ensures rapid recovery after ransomware or major incidents, preventing catastrophic downtime.
    - **Cost:** Cloud backups are usually less than $1,000 per year for SMBs.
5. **Incident Response Plan (IRP)**
    - **Why:** Provides a clear, fast response path during incidents, dramatically lowering recovery costs.

    - **Cost:** Typically a one-time setup, with minimal ongoing costs.

6. **Cyber Insurance (Basic Coverage)**
    - **Why:** Transfers financial risk of incidents. Significantly mitigates unexpected breach costs.
    - **Cost:** Typically $1,500–$5,000 per year for SMBs, depending on coverage and industry.

CEO Tip: Focus your budget first on tools and practices proven to yield high returns in breach prevention and damage reduction. Avoid spending on flashy "nice-to-haves" until core security measures are covered.

As CEO, you already make budgeting decisions that support growth, resilience, and risk management in other areas. Cybersecurity should be no different (Ponemon Institute, 2023).

You don't need to know every tool or vendor. But you do need to:

- Set the tone that security spending is strategic, not just technical
- Ask your team to prioritize outcomes over features
- Make sure spending aligns with real risks and potential consequences

Here's how to lead the conversation:

- Ask: *"What are our top three risks, and what are we doing to reduce them?"*
- Request a good-better-best security plan with pricing and expected outcomes.

- Challenge your team to identify overlapping, outdated, or underused tools

You don't need to spend like a Fortune 500 company to lead like one.

You need to know what matters and ensure it's covered.

CEO Action Checklist: Spend Smart, Not Scared

Cybersecurity doesn't need to blow your budget, but ignoring it will cost you far more. Use this checklist to align your security investments with real business value.

Get Clear on Priorities

- Ask: *"What are our top 3 risks, and what are we doing to reduce them?"*

- Focus spending on endpoint, email, finance, and client data protection first.

- Request a detailed budget breakdown from your IT team or Managed Service Provider (MSP).

Reassess What You're Already Paying For

- Review current tools for overlap, shelfware, or underuse

- Eliminate redundant or legacy tools that no longer align with risk

- Look for bundled security features in tools you already own (e.g., Microsoft 365, Google Workspace)

Think Like a Leader, Not a Technician

- Treat cybersecurity as a risk and resilience discussion, not a tech one
- Make security budgeting part of your annual and quarterly planning cycles

Revisit your budget at least once per year or after any significant security event.

Chapter 12

Creating an Incident Response Plan

That You Hope You'll Never Use

At 3:42 a.m., the CEO of a 50-person payroll services company got a call from the IT director.

"We've been hit. Our systems are down, client files are encrypted, and the ransom note is demanding $150,000 in crypto."

The CEO's first question: "Who do we call?"

The IT director didn't know.

Legal wasn't awake.

The MSP was in a different time zone.

No one could find the insurance policy.

There was no clear plan; instead, chaos prevailed.

By the time the dust settled, it wasn't just the ransom that hurt. It was the wasted time, frustrated clients, clumsy communication, and the sinking feeling that no one was steering the ship.

This chapter is about avoiding that moment.

Because when something goes wrong, and eventually, it will, you don't want to be asking, "What do we do now?"

You want to open a document, follow a plan, and lead with confidence.

When a cyber incident hits, every minute counts.

Without a plan, your team scrambles. Confusion spreads. Communication breaks down. And the cost of the breach climbs with every hour you're offline, unresponsive, or making it up as you go (IBM Security, 2023).

A well-prepared response won't erase the damage, but it will contain it.

Here's what's at risk without an incident response plan:

- **Lost Time = Lost Revenue**

Downtime affects operations, payroll, and client deliverables. The longer you delay, the higher the recovery costs will rise.

- **Decision Paralysis**

Who's in charge? Who contacts legal, insurance, or clients? Without clarity, every decision slows down, and errors multiply.

- **Client and Partner Fallout**

If you can't communicate clearly and confidently, trust erodes fast. Vague responses or slow updates damage relationships.

- **Insurance and Legal Risk**

Most cyber insurance policies require fast action and solid documentation. Regulators may also issue fines for delayed or incomplete breach notifications.

You can't build a plan during a crisis. You have to make it before you need it.

A Cyber Incident Plan Is Your Business's Fire Drill

You wouldn't wait for a fire to figure out where the exits are. You shouldn't wait for a ransomware attack to figure out who's in charge.

An incident response plan (IRP) is your company's cybersecurity playbook. It answers the critical questions before chaos sets in.

At a minimum, a strong IRP should cover:

Who to Notify, and What to Say

- Identify your internal response team, IT, leadership, legal, and external contacts, including your MSP, insurance provider, law enforcement, and PR.

- Prepare templated emails for different scenarios and audiences.

Immediate Containment Steps

- Disconnect affected systems.
- Preserve logs and evidence.
- Avoid deleting any forensic data that might be useful in an investigation.

Roles and Responsibilities

- Define who leads the response.
- Determine who will be responsible for communicating with clients, regulators, and the media.
- Assign someone to document the timeline and significant decisions.

Legal and Insurance Requirements

- Understand deadlines for breach notifications.
- Be aware of the documentation your insurance provider will require.
- Coordinate with legal or compliance counsel as needed.

A Word on Language: Say "Incident," Not "Breach"

In the early hours of a cyber event, you often won't know whether sensitive data has been accessed, exfiltrated, or exposed. That's why it's important to use the term "security incident" in your initial communications. Calling something a "breach" too early can trigger contractual obligations, regulatory reporting requirements, or legal liability, even if no data loss ultimately occurred.

An incident is any event that could compromise confidentiality, integrity, or availability of systems or data.

A breach is a confirmed incident that results in unauthorized access to protected or sensitive data.

Use neutral, accurate language early on, and always consult with legal counsel before making public statements or notifications.

Ready-to-Use Breach Notification Templates

In a crisis, clarity and speed matter. These sample templates serve as a starting point for communicating with internal staff, clients, and the public, eliminating the need to draft emails from scratch under pressure.

Each one uses neutral, professional language to describe an incident under investigation rather than a confirmed breach. Customize these based on your legal counsel's guidance and your specific obligations.

Internal Team Alert (Email or Slack)

Subject: Security Incident Under Investigation
"Our IT/security team is currently investigating a potential security incident. Please do not restart or shut down your device until further notice. More updates will follow. If you notice unusual activity, report it immediately to [security@company.com]."

Client Notification (Email)

Subject: Important: Security Incident Disclosure
"We want to inform you that our company recently identified a cybersecurity incident that may have impacted some systems. While our investigation is ongoing, we are taking immediate steps to protect your data and will share specific findings as soon as possible. We value your trust and are committed to full transparency."

Press/PR Statement

"Our organization recently detected unauthorized activity on our network. We activated our incident response procedures immediately, secured the affected systems, and engaged cybersecurity experts to assist with the investigation. Protecting our clients' and partners' data remains our highest priority."

Like a fire drill, the plan shouldn't just live in a folder. It needs to be tested. A tabletop exercise once or twice a year helps identify gaps before the real thing exposes them (CISA, 2005).

The best way to stay calm in a crisis? Rehearse when things are quiet.

After every actual incident or practice drill, update the plan to reflect what worked and what didn't. Think of continuous improvement as part of your ongoing response strategy (NIST, 2025).

You don't need a 100-page binder to respond effectively.

When a breach happens, what you need most is clarity in the first 30 minutes. The following one-page cheat sheet provides your leadership team with an at-a-glance guide to take immediate, coordinated action, even before the full incident response plan is opened. Print it. Post it. Review it quarterly. Because during a crisis, simplicity saves time, and time saves trust.

Incident Response Cheat Sheet

First 30 Minutes (Immediate Response)

- Disconnect infected systems from the network
- Do not reboot or delete files
- Notify the internal IR team or MSP
- Begin documenting key actions and timestamps

Key Contacts

- IT Lead: ____________________
- CEO/Exec Contact: ____________________
- MSP Contact: ____________________
- Cyber Insurer: ____________________
- Legal Counsel: ____________________

Initial Containment Actions

- Identify affected systems and users
- Secure email and admin credentials
- Preserve system logs and files for forensics

External Notifications

- Clients (if affected): Send within 24–72 hrs
- Regulators (if required): Follow compliance timeframes
- Insurer: Notify within a policy-required window

CEO Tip: Have a printed copy of this next to your company's incident response plan, not just in the cloud. When the network's down, this still works.

Your Job Is to Lead, Not to Improvise

When a cyber incident hits, everyone looks to you for clarity, direction, and confidence. Without a plan, you'll be making high-stakes decisions under pressure, with little time and even less certainty.

Your job isn't to fix the breach. It's to lead the response.

Here's what that means:

Know the Plan Exists

- Ask for a copy of your company's IRP.
- If it doesn't exist, make its creation a priority this quarter.

Know Your Role

- Are you the final decision-maker on ransom payments?
- Will you speak directly to clients or delegate that task?
- Do you have contact information for your cyber insurer and legal counsel?

Lead the Communication

- Silence or vague messaging damages trust.
- A clear, steady voice, both internally and externally, can preserve relationships and guide your team through chaos.
- You don't need to have all the answers.
- You need to ask the right questions before the worst day of your career starts at 3 a.m.

CEO Action Checklist: Build the Plan Before You Need It

You can't stop every incident, but you **can** control how your business responds.

Use this checklist to make sure your team isn't caught off guard.

Create or Review Your Incident Response Plan (IRP)

- Ask: *"Do we have a documented cyber incident response plan?"*
- Confirm that it includes roles, contacts (both internal and external), and action steps.
- Schedule a tabletop test to walk through a realistic scenario.

Assign Clear Roles and Responsibilities

- Who leads the response?
- Who communicates with clients, the media, and regulators?
- Who contacts legal and insurance?

Ensure Visibility and Readiness

- Ensure that all leadership is aware of where to find the plan.
- Rehearse it annually or after any significant tech change.
- Treat it like a fire drill: quick, precise, and practiced.

Chapter 13

The Future of Cyber Risk

In 2021, a ransomware group called DarkSide crippled the Colonial Pipeline, one of the largest fuel suppliers in the United States, causing gas shortages across the East Coast.

But here's what made the attack especially concerning:

The group didn't build the ransomware; they licensed it.

They utilized a model called Ransomware-as-a-Service (RaaS), in which criminal developers create ransomware kits and sell or rent them to others. The affiliates run the attacks, and the developers get a percentage of the ransom.

Now, imagine that model combined with AI-powered phishing emails, fake voice messages, and real-time data analysis. That future isn't five years away. It's already here.

This chapter looks ahead at the trends shaping the next wave of cyber threats and what small and midsize business leaders like me need to prepare for now.

The tools criminals use are evolving faster than any firewall, and this time, they scale like software.

Cybercrime has evolved from isolated hacking to a full-scale criminal enterprise. It now includes business models, affiliate programs, help desks, revenue sharing, and, increasingly, artificial intelligence.

The barrier to entry is gone. You don't need technical skills to launch an attack anymore, just a credit card and an internet connection.

Here's what that means for all of us:

- **More Attacks, More Often**

Ransomware-as-a-service enables low-skilled criminals to target hundreds of businesses simultaneously.

We're not just dealing with lone hackers anymore; we're facing organized, repeatable tactics from people running a criminal franchise model.

- **AI-Driven Social Engineering**

AI now writes convincing phishing emails with perfect grammar and no obvious red flags.

It can mimic the tone of your CFO, create fake voicemails, and generate counterfeit invoices that match those of your authentic vendors.

- **Supply Chain Risk**

Attackers may not target you directly; instead, they'll use you to reach your clients or vendors.

A single compromised email or shared file can create a domino effect across multiple businesses.

- **Deepfakes and Data Manipulation**

We're approaching a point where attackers will use synthetic voice and video to impersonate team members or executives.

They may also poison AI systems with misleading data to influence decisions or disrupt automated processes.

This isn't just about protecting our businesses anymore.

It's about protecting the trust others place in us, our relationships, our reputation, and even our sense of what's real.

What's Real vs. Hype in Emerging Cyber Threats

Emerging Threat	Real Risk (Now)	Hype Factor	What to Watch	CEO Takeaway
AI-Powered Phishing	Yes	Moderate	Targeted, convincing scams using public data	Train your team on modern, AI-shaped scams
Deepfake Audio/Video	Emerging	High	CEO voice fakes, fake Zoom calls	Confirm unusual requests via a second channel
Quantum Decryption	Not Yet	Very High	Decades away from breaking current encryption	Monitor, don't panic, post-quantum crypto is in progress
Ransomware-as-a-Service	Yes	Low	Toolkits sold on the dark web	Assume attackers don't need skills, just budget
AI-Generated Malware	Experimental	Moderate	Custom code that mutates and evades detection	Invest in endpoint protection + detection/response

CEO Tip: The danger isn't in the headline; it's in the everyday blind spot. Focus on what's here now and gaining traction, not just the buzzwords.

Cybercrime Now Moves at the Speed of Software

What once required weeks of planning and deep technical skill can now be accomplished in minutes using rented tools and AI automation.

Cyberattacks have become scalable, repeatable, and alarmingly efficient. And just like modern software companies, cybercriminals are:

- Automating everything: phishing, reconnaissance, even ransom negotiations
- Outsourcing complex tasks through marketplaces and subscription kits
- Targeting small and midsize businesses with mass attacks using low-cost, high-return tools

As business leaders, here's what this shift means for us:

Cyber risk is now a constant threat

- It's no longer about an annual audit; it's something we face every day.
- Our defenses need to adapt in real time, not on a quarterly cycle.

AI is giving attackers a serious advantage

- The once-prominent scams have evolved into polished, professional, and highly personalised ones.
- Gone are the days of broken English and poor formatting; AI has erased those telltale signs.

If you're connected, you're a target

- Every cloud app, integration, and exposed endpoint increases your attack surface.
- A single compromised user or misconfigured system can open the door.

Your risk isn't based on your size or your industry anymore; it's based on your digital footprint.

This isn't hype. It's math. Currently, the math favors the attacker.

If You're Waiting to Catch Up, You're Already Behind

Technology continues to accelerate, and risk is keeping pace with it.

As a CEO, I look forward to new regulations or products that will make us safer. I have to lead with urgency because the criminals already are.

Here's how I'm approaching it and how other forward-thinking CEOs are, too:

Treat cyber risk like business risk

- I don't just ask if our systems are secure; I ask how fast they can detect and respond.
- Cyber risk now has a seat at the table in strategic planning, vendor decisions, and boardroom conversations.

Invest in people, not just products

- No single tool can stop an AI-crafted phishing attack. My team needs to be trained, alert, and empowered to act.
- Resilience matters more than perfection: detect quickly, respond fast, and communicate clearly.

Stay ahead of what's next

- I regularly ask our IT leads, "What are we doing to prepare for

AI-driven threats?"

- I push for constant improvement, not one-time fixes.
- And I'm exploring cyber resilience assessments that look beyond prevention to how quickly we can recover.

The companies that will survive the next wave of threats aren't just the ones spending more.

They're the ones leading early before they're forced to react late.

CEO Action Checklist: Prepare for What's Coming, Not Just What's Familiar

The threats are evolving. Your strategy should, too. Use this checklist to stay ahead of the next wave of cyber risk.

Stay Informed and Proactive

- Ask your team: *"How are we preparing for AI-powered phishing and automation-based attacks?"*
- Request quarterly briefings on emerging threats, not just current tools and technologies.

Shift Your Focus to Resilience

- Ensure you can detect and respond quickly, not just block threats.
- Simulate what would happen if an attacker got past your defenses: *How long until we know? Who does what?*

Empower People, Not Just Technology

- Train your team on modern social engineering tactics, not just basic phishing.
- Reinforce a culture where reporting near-misses is celebrated, not punished.

Lead with a Future-Ready Mindset

- Include cyber risk in leadership, finance, and client planning conversations.
- Consider scheduling a tabletop exercise that includes an AI-generated threat scenario.

Chapter 14

Your Cybersecurity Roadmap

The First 90 Days

After reading a cybersecurity report about the rise in ransomware and phishing attacks, the CEO of a 35-person professional services firm asked the one question I hear most often:

"Where do we start?"

They had a managed IT provider, antivirus software, and a basic cyber insurance policy but lacked a clear understanding of what was working, what was missing, or what to do next.

Sound familiar?

Most CEOs don't need more data. They need a starting point,a clear, confident plan to shift from a reactive to a proactive approach.

That's what this chapter offers:

A 90-day roadmap to make your business meaningfully more secure, without jargon, sales pitches, or bloated checklists.

This is about real progress. Fast.

The first 90 days of any new initiative set the tone for the project. Cybersecurity is no different.

If you put it off, you risk:

Lingering Vulnerabilities

- Employees clicking on phishing emails
- Systems left unpatched and exposed
- Former staff or vendors with access they shouldn't have

Compounded Risk Exposure

- Insurance claims denied over missing controls
- Compliance gaps regulators won't ignore
- Small issues escalate into major incidents

Leadership Blind Spots

- No clear picture of what's protected
- No accountability between departments
- No confidence you're genuinely prepared

You don't have to fix everything today.

But doing nothing keeps your risk exactly where it is, or worse.

The following 90 days are your chance to build momentum.

To show your team and your board that cybersecurity isn't just IT's job. It's a leadership priority.

Progress Beats Perfection

You don't need a five-year roadmap to make an impact.

You need clarity, focus, and follow-through, especially in your first 90 days (NIST, 2022).

Cybersecurity is about doing the most important things first. Start by focusing on three areas:

1. People

Your employees are your front line and your most significant risk.

Begin with phishing training, cleaning up access controls, and clearly outlining the process for reporting suspicious activity.

2. Systems

Secure the critical systems that keep your business running:

Email, file sharing, financial platforms, and client data. Add MFA, set up reliable backups, and make sure endpoint protection is active.

3. Planning

If something goes wrong tomorrow, what happens?

Ensure you have a basic incident response plan and understand precisely what your cyber insurance covers and what it doesn't.

This 90-day plan helps you move quickly without wasting time or money on things that don't matter yet.

You won't solve everything. But by next quarter, you'll be measurably safer and leading from a place of clarity, not chaos.

Security Progress Starts with Leadership

The most secure companies didn't get there by buying the most expensive tools.

They got there because leadership made cybersecurity a priority and followed through.

You don't need to be a technical expert.

You don't need to handle it all yourself.

But you do need to move the initiative forward.

Here's how:

Set the Direction

- Make it clear that cybersecurity is not optional, and it's not just IT's responsibility.
- Announce a 90-day push for progress and connect it to business risk and client trust.

Assign Ownership

- Whether it's your MSP, IT lead, or operations manager, someone must own the roadmap.

- Set regular check-ins and ask: "What's done, what's in progress, and what's holding us up?"

Measure What Matters

- Don't settle for vague updates like "We installed more tools."
- Ask the fundamental question: Are we more protected than we were 30 days ago?

The most potent cybersecurity tool in your company isn't a product.

It's your leadership.

CEO Action Checklist: Your 90-Day Cybersecurity Sprint

You don't need perfection. You need progress.

Use this 90-day checklist to drive momentum, reduce risk, and lead with confidence.

Week 1–2: Establish Ownership and Baseline

- Appoint someone to own the 90-day security roadmap (internal or external)
- Request a brief "state of security" report, including MFA status, backups, access control, and phishing training.
- Announce to your team: *"Cybersecurity is a business priority, and we're taking action now."*

Week 3–6: Lock Down the Basics

- Enable MFA on all critical systems (email, file sharing, finance, admin tools) (CISA, 2023)
- Install or confirm endpoint protection on all company devices.
- Ensure offsite, tested backups are in place for business-critical data.

Week 7–10: Train and Clean Up Access

- Schedule phishing training for all staff (Proofpoint, 2023)
- Review who has access to what, and remove anything unnecessary
- Review and update vendor and contractor access.

Week 11–12: Plan for a Breach

- Create or review your incident response plan.
- Confirm contact info for IT, legal, insurance, and communications.

Schedule a basic tabletop test: *"What would we do if we got hit tomorrow?"*

What to Do After the First 90 Days

If you've completed the first 90 days, congrats. You've established momentum, closed major gaps, and taken cybersecurity from assumption to action.

Now, it's time to build on that foundation.

The next 90 days aren't about new checklists. They're about maturing your security posture, reinforcing good habits, and preparing for what's next.

Here's what that looks like.

Your Next 90 Days Cybersecurity Roadmap

Weeks	Focus Area	Actions
13–16	**Audit and Optimize**	• Conduct a full-access audit • Review tools for overlap or gaps
17–20	**Policy and Documentation**	• Formalize security policies (MFA, backups, incident response) • Create a cybersecurity handbook or training guide
21–24	**Test and Improve**	• Run a phishing simulation • Do a tabletop breach exercise • Review cyber insurance policy and update if needed

Final Thoughts

Security Is a Journey, and Leadership Drives It

You don't need to become a cybersecurity expert.

You don't need to understand every tool, tactic, or threat.

But you do need to lead.

Cybersecurity isn't just a technical issue; it's a business responsibility.

And today, it's also a mark of strong leadership.

The most successful companies aren't the ones that never get attacked.

They're the ones who prepare, respond, and recover quickly and clearly because leadership made security a priority.

If you've read this far, you're already ahead.

Now it's time to:

- Ask smarter questions
- Make confident decisions
- Empower your team

- Own the risk
- Build a culture that treats security as part of how you do business

You don't need to do everything at once.

Start with the 90-day roadmap in Chapter 12.

Revisit the CEO Action Checklists throughout the book.

Contact your IT team or Managed Service Provider (MSP).

Focus on real-world readiness, not perfect theory.

And if you need support?

We offer consultations, playbooks, and done-for-you security reviews tailored for small and midsize business leaders.

Visit: https://inventivehq.com

Because cybersecurity isn't something you wait for.

It's something you lead.

About the author

Sean Conroy is a seasoned technology leader, virtual Chief Information Security Officer (CISO), and founder of **Inventive HQ**. This cybersecurity and cloud consulting firm helps small and mid-sized businesses stay secure, resilient, and audit-ready, without the complexity of enterprise solutions.

With over 20 years of experience across various industries, including finance, healthcare, legal, and Transportation, Sean has led IT and security programs at high-growth startups, public companies, and mission-critical service providers. He's advised CEOs, board members, and operational teams on everything from ransomware recovery to building practical, budget-conscious security programs that work.

Before launching Inventive HQ, Sean served as the technology leader at multiple firms, where he built out infrastructure, led security audits, and helped leadership teams align technology decisions with business goals. He's also been on the other side of the table, helping teams rebuild after breaches, audit failures, and compliance gaps that were overlooked until it was too late.

Today, Sean helps organizations:

- Understand and reduce their cybersecurity risk

- Build security roadmaps they can follow.
- Navigate vendor noise, insurance confusion, and regulatory complexity.
- Prepare for tomorrow's threats without losing focus on today's business.

He believes that **security should be led from the top**, made simple for everyone, and measured by business impact, not just technical checklists.

Sean lives in California with his family and is a frequent speaker, writer, and consultant on cybersecurity for small to medium-sized businesses (SMBs). You can connect with him at LinkedIn.com/in/spconroy

Resources

Reports and Industry Surveys

Coveware. (2023, July 21). *Ransom monetization rates fall to record low despite jump in average ransom payments*. https://www.coveware.com/blog/2023/7/21/ransom-monetization-rates-fall-to-record-low-despite-jump-in-average-ransom-payments

Coveware. (2024, April 17). *RaaS devs hurt their credibility by cheating affiliates in Q1 2024*. https://www.coveware.com/blog/2024/4/17/raas-devs-hurt-their-credibility-by-cheating-affiliates-in-q1-2024

CrowdStrike. (2023). *Global threat report*. https://www.crowdstrike.com/global-threat-report/

Gartner. (2023). *Third-party risk management and vendor security expectations*. https://www.gartner.com/en/legal-compliance/trends/tprm-benchmarking-report

Gartner. (2024). *Third-party risk management (TPRM): An essential guide*. https://www.gartner.com/en/legal-compliance/topics/third-party-risk-management-tprm

IBM Security. (2023). *Cost of a data breach report*. https://www.ibm.com/reports/data-breach

Microsoft. (2023). *Cyber Signals: AI and the future of threats*. https://www.microsoft.com/en-us/security/blog/2024/02/14/cyber-signals-navigating-cyberthreats-and-strengthening-defenses-in-the-era-of-ai/

Microsoft. (2023). *SMB cybersecurity playbook*. https://download.microsoft.com/download/9/c/1/9c167271-8209-492e-acc2-38a39d1834c2/m365bp-cybersecurity-playbook.pdf

Microsoft Blog. (2022). *MFA: The basics, and why it works*. https://techcommunity.microsoft.com/blog/microsoft-entra-blog/your-paword-doesnt-matter/731984

Microsoft Blog. (2023, May 31). *XDR meets IAM: Comprehensive identity threat detection and response with Microsoft*. https://www.microsoft.com/enus/security/blog/2023/05/31/xdr-meets-iam-comprehensive-identity-threat-detection-and-response-with-microsoft/

Microsoft Digital Defense Report. (2023). *The rise of cybercrime-as-a-service*. https://www.microsoft.com/en-us/security/security-insider/microsoft-digital-defense-report-2023

National Cybersecurity Alliance. (2022). *Cybersecurity: 3 things every small business owner should know*. https://www.staysafeonline.org/articles/cybersecurity-3-things-every-small-business-owner-should-know

National Cybersecurity Alliance. (2023). *2023 Cybersecurity Small Business Report.* https://www.staysafeonline.org/press/small-midsized-businesses-protect-digital-assets

National Cybersecurity Alliance. (2023). *Cybersecurity for SMBs: NCA annual report.* https://www.staysafeonline.org/articles/how-cyber-education-for-employees-safeguards-your-business

NIST. (2022). *Cybersecurity framework.* https://www.nist.gov/cyberframework

NIST. (2022). *Small business cybersecurity quick wins guide.* https://www.nist.gov/itl/smallbusinesscyber

NIST. (2022). *Small business cybersecurity corner.* https://www.nist.gov/itl/smallbusinesscyber

NIST. (2025). *Computer security incident handling guide (SP 800-61 Rev. 3).* https://csrc.nist.gov/pubs/sp/800/61/r3/final

NIST. (2020). *Workforce framework for cybersecurity (NICE Framework), NIST Special Publication 800-181 Revision 1.* https://nvlpubs.nist.gov/nistpubs/specialpublications/nist.sp.800-181.pdf

Palo Alto Networks Unit 42. (2023). *Ransomware and extortion report.* https://www.paloaltonetworks.com/resources/research/2023-unit42-ransomware-extortion-report

Ponemon Institute. (2023). *Cost of insider threats: Global report.* https://ponemonsullivanreport.com/2023/10/cost-of-insider-risks-global-report-2023/

Proofpoint. (2023). *State of the phish report.* https://www.proofpoint.com/us/resources/threat-reports/state-of-phish

Proofpoint. (2024). *Generative AI risks: What your people should know.* https://www.proofpoint.com/us/blog/security-awareness-training/generative-ai-risks-to-know

SANS Institute. (2023). *Leveraging the SANS Security Awareness Maturity Model to effectively manage human risk.* https://assets.contentstack.io/v3/assets/blt36c2e63521272fdc/blt0cde11556a4cb9e1/6570e05a302a16eb7a46905e/SANS_ebook_security_awareness_maturity_model_v3.pdf

Stanford University & Tessian. (2022). *The psychology of human error.* https://f.hubspotusercontent20.net/hubfs/1670277/%5BCollateral%5D%20Tessian-Research-Reports/%5BTessian%20Research%5D%20Psychology%20of%20Human%20Error%202022.pdf

Techaisle. (2025). *Techaisle research shows shifts in SMB and midmarket security investment trends.* https://techaisle.com/blog/570-techaisle-research-shows-shifts-in-smb-and-midmarket-security-investment-trends

Techtarget. (2022). *Cybersecurity budget breakdown and best practices.* https://www.techtarget.com/searchsecurity/tip/Cybersecurity-budget-breakdown-and-best-practices

Verizon. (2023). *Data breach investigations report (DBIR)*. https://www.verizon.com/business/resources/reports/dbir/

Verizon. (2024). *2024 data breach investigations report (DBIR)*. https://www.verizon.com/business/resources/reports/dbir/

Verizon. (2025). *2024 data breach investigations report (DBIR)*. https://www.verizon.com/business/resources/reports/dbir/

Welle, E. (2021, June 21). Scripps Health says ransomware attack costs top $112.7 million. *San Diego Union-Tribune*. https://www.sandiegouniontribune.com/news/health/story/2021-06-21/scripps-health-ransomware-attack-costs

Government and Regulatory Sources

CISA (Cybersecurity & Infrastructure Security Agency). (2023). *Known exploited vulnerabilities catalog*. https://www.cisa.gov/known-exploited-vulnerabilities-catalog

CISA (Cybersecurity & Infrastructure Security Agency). (2023). *Cyber essentials for small businesses*. https://www.cisa.gov/cyber-essentials

CISA (Cybersecurity & Infrastructure Security Agency). (2023). *Incident response planning guide*. [Link truncated]

CISA (Cybersecurity & Infrastructure Security Agency). (2025). *Incident response tabletop exercise packages*. https://www.cisa.gov/resources-tools/services/cisa-tabletop-exercise-packages

CISA. (2023). *Securing the software supply chain*. https://www.cisa.gov/resources-tools/resources/securing-software-supply-chain-recommended-practices-guide-customers-and

CISA Fact Sheet. (n.d.). *Implementing phishing-resistant MFA*. https://www.cisa.gov/sites/default/files/publications/fact-sheet-implementing-phishing-resistant-mfa-508c.pdf

FBI Internet Crime Complaint Center (IC3). (2022). *Internet crime report 2022*. https://www.ic3.gov/AnnualReport/Reports/2022_ic3report.pdf

FBI Internet Crime Complaint Center (IC3). (2022). *Business email compromise: The $2.7 billion scam*. https://www.fbi.gov/how-we-can-help-you/scams-and-safety/common-frauds-and-scams/business-email-compromise

U.S. Department of Health and Human Services (HHS). (2023). *Enforcement highlights*. https://www.hhs.gov/hipaa/for-professionals/compliance-enforcement/data

U.S. Department of Justice. (2021). *DarkSide ransomware attack on Colonial Pipeline*. https://www.justice.gov/archives/opa/speech/dag-monaco-delivers-remarks-press-conference-darkside-attack-colonial-pipeline

Additional Notable Sources

Insureon. (2025). *What are the minimum requirements for cybersecurity insurance?* https://www.insureon.com/small-business-insurance/cyber-liability/requirements

Coalition Inc. (2023). *Cyber insurance claims report: Mid-year update.* https://www.coalitioninc.com/announcements/2023-claims-report-mid-year-update

Coalition Inc. (2023). *Cyber claims report – mid-year update.* https://web.coalitioninc.com/download-2023-cyber-claims-report-mid-year-update.html

www.ingramcontent.com/pod-product-compliance
Lightning Source LLC
LaVergne TN
LVHW090409210926
848480LV00002B/517